DID YOU THINK *TO* PRAY?

TRUE ACCOUNTS *OF THE* POWER *OF* PRAYER

DID YOU THINK TO PRAY?

TRUE ACCOUNTS OF THE POWER OF PRAYER

THEDA SHOWALTER WASHBURN

HORIZON PUBLISHERS
AN IMPRINT OF CEDAR FORT, INC.
SPRINGVILLE, UTAH

ISBN 13: 978-0-88290-678-2

Published by Horizon Publishers, an imprint of Cedar Fort, Inc.
2373 W. 700 S., Springville, UT 84663
Distributed by Cedar Fort, Inc., www.cedarfort.com

Cover design by Rebecca J. Greenwood
Cover design © 2012 by Lyle Mortimer

Printed in the United States of America

10 9 8 7 6 5 4 3 2 1

Contents

Preface

It is amazing that people's lives can change as from night to day once they humble themselves, put off the "natural man," accept Christ as their Savior and strive to live His gospel. I've seen this happen time and time again as these great, sincere, and humble spiritual experiences and testimonies testify.

The decision to gather these testimonies and write this book came after I heard the testimonies of Brother Craig Caldwell and Brother Bud Covington at a meeting of our Family Home Evening group. Brother Caldwell had been a worldly man, totally inactive, and Brother Covington had been a non-member. The testimonies of their conversions and the great changes that came into their lives so touched me, and all the people who were present, that I decided to try to find others who had accepted the gospel and changed their lives. Over many years of searching I found amazing, sincere testimonies which brought tears to my eyes as I recorded them.

I'm grateful to have had the opportunity to know these strong, humble people. Many of them have overcome terrible addictions and other problems by prayer and repentance and are now servants of the Lord. Others gave choice spiritual experiences that had brought them understanding and comfort.

These experiences prove the power of prayer. I hope and pray that these accounts may help those who are struggling find strength to overcome their problems and realize that with the help of God, anything is possible.

Put God First

This is the amazing story of Craig Caldwell's great spiritual journey. The Lord first stripped him of worldly riches, causing him to be humble and prayerful and to plead for God's help. He then visited him and, "in the twinkling of an eye," cleansed his body and cured his horrible addictions of fifty years. Since that time, Craig has lost all desire for those drugs, nicotine and alcohol, and completely turned his life around.

I've been asked to tell of some experiences and problems I've had in my life, and how, through the power and mercy of our Heavenly Father, I've been able to overcome them. I do this humbly, in the hope I may be able to help others who are struggling with similar problems, that they too may overcome them and find the joy and peace I've found.

I was born on the Ute Indian reservation in Deep Creek, Utah, of good LDS parents. My mother was one of the first missionaries from that area so I was brought up in the Church. I was baptized in the canal, for that was our only facility at that time.

I remember well when we built the new chapel. It was done with extreme hardship on the members as they had to do most of the work and pay most of the bills. We built a nice building. About the only recreation we had was playing basketball and dancing, and oh, how I loved that!

Due to several events that happened when I was about fourteen and the fact that I was rebellious, I left the Church and went on my merry way for some 50-odd years. During that period of time I traveled all over the country meeting all kinds of people. I was also breaking many of the Lord's commandments I'd been taught as a boy. This way of living carried on through two failed marriages. I attribute much of their failure to my dissolute way of life.

I became interested in the oil business, and through this I met Robert (Bud) Covington, a brilliant geologist. We became partners and had good success in our business ventures for many years, to the point of having our own successful oil company, Hiko Bell, on the stock market. Everything we touched turned to gold—liquid gold, oil. We were able to bring in many oil wells. This success continued for years, for Bud, the geologist, had a "nose" for oil. Then our luck changed completely, and everything we tried failed. Businessmen I trusted took advantage of me and seemed to be dishonest. I seemed unable to make anything change. I had no direction.

I watched in shocked disbelief as my little empire crumbled before my eyes! All the assets, the oil wells, the airplanes, the boats, the Cadillacs, the big home, all disappeared while I stood helplessly by. I was virtually left without any material wealth. Since I had lived entirely for material things, I felt my whole life was over. To make matters worse, my wife, whom I adored, divorced me.

Even though I was at the "bottom of the barrel," I always found enough money to buy cigarettes and liquor. I realize now that losing my wealth was God's way of humbling me and bringing me back to Him.

My son, Jimmie, had followed in my footsteps for some time, partying and drinking. Due to the influence of his dear wife and her parents, he turned his life around. He was most desirous that I do the same, but my addictions were so ingrained after all those years that even the thought of living without my cigarettes and liquor was unthinkable.

Because I had always loved animals, I moved to a farm out in the country to lick my wounds and worry about my enormous debt. I felt I was in a black hole that I would never be able to climb out of. My life seemed empty and when my money disappeared, so did many of my fair-weather friends.

For some unexplainable reason, I started attending the LDS Church in the Naples Ward. While I was in the chapel I felt a calmness and peace I hadn't enjoyed in years.

There was a grand man in the ward named Clawson Elliott. He told the bishop he wanted me as his home-teaching companion. I'm sure the Bishop objected for my life-style was well known, but Clawson persisted. He finally came to me and asked me to be his teaching companion. I immediately told him that I wasn't worthy of such a job as I smoked and drank. He said he knew that, but he wanted me anyway. He said, "You'll quit, and someday you'll go to the Temple." I told him he was a dreamer, but I went home teaching with him anyway. I didn't try to teach, nor did he ask me to, but I listened to the discussions between him and the humble, wonderful people that we visited. I often wondered how those people could have such strong, unshakable testimonies and I began to ponder this in my heart. I also began to love them as I did Clawson.

I often told him that because of my addictions, I didn't belong in church, but he said that we go to church to help us overcome our problems and that not everyone in church is perfect. He said, "Many are here for the same reason you're here, even though they might have different problems."

The feeling of warmth and fellowship I felt in that ward is difficult to describe. I felt totally accepted and loved. I'd go to church for three hours and during that time, I had no desire to smoke or drink, but the second I touched that door, I became frantic to rush home and have a drink and a smoke. If I got in my car and it didn't start immediately, I panicked because my addictions were so strong. I continued to go to church and felt calm and happy there. Afterward, I'd hurry home in a frenzy.

Norman Haslem was the Bishop at the time, and he is a man of God. One day he said, "Craig, I'd like to ordain you a priest." (I'd left the Church at 14 as a Teacher). I said, "Bishop, I appreciate the kindness and fellowship all of you good people have shown me, but I can't change. I simply don't have the strength to stop my bad habits and addictions. I don't feel I'm worthy."

Finally, after he'd persisted for some time, I said "All right, I'd like all of the Priesthood holders to put their hands on my head good and tight, for it is a hard head, and I'd like you to give me a blessing." He gave me a wonderful blessing. I could feel the power of the Priesthood there, but when I returned home, I still had this terrible urge to drink and smoke. Although I prayed for strength continually, I couldn't stop, though I knew my lifestyle was killing me.

Every morning I'd have a horrible hangover. I needed a handful of aspirin, a bottle of Pepto-Bismol, a couple of Alka-Seltzers, a lot of Tums and a whole pot of black coffee to even get going. If any of you have ever drunk a fifth of whiskey and smoked three packs of cigarettes a day as I did for over forty years, you know how upsetting it is to your system. Around four every afternoon, my body was literally screaming for a drink. I was an absolute slave to those pernicious addictions! My habits told me what to do and I helplessly obeyed!

One morning I was sitting on the side of the bed with a terrible hangover. I felt weak and ill as I prayed. "Oh, Lord, am I going to have to go through this every morning for the rest of my life? Please give me the strength to stop these terrible habits." Then a miracle happened. It seemed as if the Lord Himself came to me and put his arm around my shoulder and said, "You'll never want to drink or smoke again."

I was amazed and shocked at the miraculous answer to my prayers. I'd been promised by the Lord that I'd be free of addictions, yet I knew how powerful they were and I wondered what would happen when four o'clock, my drinking time, came.

At four o'clock, my stomach was utterly calm! I had no desire to smoke, or drink, even coffee, and haven't to this day. I also have not taken a Tums or anything else to settle my stomach. God cleansed my system of the desire for cigarettes and liquor and the poisons they had put into my body, in the twinkling of an eye. I felt free for the first time in years! How overjoyed and grateful to the Lord I was and am!

I couldn't have quit those terrible habits alone, but when you have God as your partner you can do anything! There is no way that I could have stopped even one bad habit by myself, and yet, with God's help, I'd quit three: smoking, drinking and coffee all at once with no after-effects or withdrawal symptoms. All desire for them had left. To me this was a miracle! We are supposed to be able to have revelation for our personal affairs, and this was indeed a great revelation to me.

A few of my former drinking buddies heard I had quit drinking so they came to the house determined to get me to go to a drinking party with them. They said they'd heard I'd quit drinking but they didn't believe I had. I told them I had quit, but I hadn't done it, the Lord had taken away all desire for liquor and cigarettes from me. I had Him alone to thank for this miracle! They poured whiskey before me and had a difficult time believing me when I told them that I had no desire to ever drink or smoke again. When they found I was unshakable, they left and have never returned. *I now had a testimony that God lives and answers prayers. I knew he did, for he'd surely answered mine in a miraculous way!*

One hot Saturday, I had been out to Red Wash looking at some oil wells. When I returned, there was a note from my daughter saying that she, her husband, and children were going to the mountain fishing that weekend and wanted me to join them. She knew how much I loved to fish, and to be with her and my grandchildren. It was also lovely and cool on the mountain. I was so hot and tired I decided I'd wait and go to the mountain the next day. Because of my recent business failures and the dishonest partners who'd cheated me, I felt that people had pushed me around and I decided that I was going to do what I wanted to do for a change. I was going fishing with my daughter and grandchildren even if it was Sunday.

That Sunday morning as I showered, I began to wonder how people ever gained such strong, unshakable testimonies of the gospel as I'd witnessed on my home-teaching route. I deeply desired such a testimony. I wanted to know if the Church was true so I began to pray. I asked God if Joseph Smith was a true prophet and if the LDS Church was the true church. "If this is the true Church, do you want me to be active in the Church? What do you want me to do? Please, God, give me some direction, some sign. Let me know in some way."

Just then the phone rang. I wrapped a towel around me and answered it. It was Ralph Dart, a member of our Bishopric. He said that the Bishop wanted to see me that morning. I couldn't tell him I was going fishing so I told him that I was too busy to go to church that day. Brother Dart is a determined man. He kept me on the phone for about ten minutes trying to get me to commit to attend church that morning. As I hung up the phone, I congratulated myself thinking, " Well, he thought he was going to get me, but I got away." Then a clear voice said, "You asked me to let you know if the Church was true—to send you a message in some way and I did, and you forgot your request from the shower to the phone." It was true. I'd asked for direction and for a testimony that the Church was true. I'd received a call from the Lord, and had forgotten what I'd been praying for. Right then I vowed to put God number one in my life.

I went to church as quickly as I've ever done anything in my life! If I could have gone in my towel, I would have—so great was my desire to get there, for I knew who was sending me! I kept wondering what in the world the Bishop wanted. Bishop Haslem greeted me and asked me if I'd like to teach the Blazer boys in Primary. I hadn't been to Primary in 50 years but I immediately said "yes," for I knew why I was there and that God had sent me. He said, "You can have a few days to think it over." I said, "Bishop, I don't have to think it over. I know who sent me here and I'm going to do whatever He and you ask of me. I don't know what I'm going to teach those boys, but I'll learn." I then started on a job which lasted five years and was one of the most rewarding experiences of my life.

That group of boys was considered the hardest to handle of any in the ward. One of them, according to their previous teacher, was incorrigible. I soon found out what the teacher meant. Joe was the ring-leader of a rough bunch of boys, and a terrible handful. One day I'd had enough of his disrupting the class so I grabbed him by the seat of the pants and out we went into the hall. I was angry, but the Lord had sent the Bishop of another ward into the hall for a purpose right at that crucial moment. He said, "Craig, what's the problem?" in a calm voice. I told him I'd had enough of that kid and was throwing him out of the class. He asked me to give Joe another chance. When we returned to the classroom, there wasn't another sound out of any of the boys or from Joe. Those boys were just wonderful and respectful from then on. Joe became one of my best friends, as did the rest of the fellows in that class. I took them camping and fishing and they loved it. We developed a very close relationship and I began to love them as much as I did my own son. When I entered the chapel they'd come up and put their arms around me. I still get cards of thanks and appreciation from Joe. He says I turned his life around. I feel the Lord sent me there to help him. He is a choice young man. All of those young fellows are active in the Church and are great boys and I love them!

I now not only know that there is a God who hears and answers prayers, but that the Church of Jesus Christ is true. This testimony is priceless to me!

The Lord had blessed me with the gospel and my animals on my little farm, and I was thankful for those blessings. I had never been in debt before, but now I had an enormous debt hanging over my head. That worried me. However, I was helpless to solve it. I also lacked one thing in my personal life. I needed a good wife—a companion to share my life with. I kept praying for someone to love me even though I was getting old and was broke financially. Then another great miracle came into my life!

One day my partner, Bud, brought a young woman to our office to keep the books. Her name was Jennifer Hatch. She had been married to a doctor, and they became the parents of five children and then divorced. She was a good member of the Church.

When Jennifer found the true state of our company's financial affairs—that we were not only broke, but that there was a million dollars worth of judgments against us at twelve percent interest—she was horrified and immediately took action!

Even though I was innocent of any wrong-doing, I had been unable to employ a lawyer for I had nothing with which to pay one. Jennifer came from a very well-connected and prominent family. She immediately called her uncle, John Paul Stevens, who is on the Supreme Court. He told her Sandra Day O'Connor would be in Provo to give a talk at Brigham Young University that very week and he'd make an appointment for Jennifer to meet with her and Rex Lee, President of Brigham Young University. He felt sure that they would find a lawyer who would take our case.

Jennifer rushed to Provo and gave those important people the true facts. They could see that I wasn't to blame for the financial bind we were in. President Lee and Mrs. O'Connor found a great lawyer to take our case. What a blessing that was to me, for I had given up trying to find a lawyer, and the fact that he managed to have all those crushing judgments against us dismissed was indeed a miracle! What a blessing! Even if I was left with nothing, I no longer cared, for I was free from that heavy burden!

I believe that Jennifer was sent to our office as a direct answer to my fervent prayers. Who else in the world would have had the connections she had, or the courage to go out and meet with a member of the Supreme Court and the President of a great university and plead my case? She'd found that I'd never signed documents that would incriminate me. My partner, an honest man, had been duped by terribly dishonest men and signed papers he should never have signed. How grateful I am to her for untangling the terrible web that bound us.

In spite of the great difference in our ages, Jennifer and I fell deeply in love. Together we are raising her children, and now my life is complete. Even though I don't have many material possessions, they simply don't matter any more. I have the two most important things in life—a testimony of the Gospel of Jesus Christ and the love of a good woman. I wouldn't trade my testimony for all the riches in the world! I feel that I'm now living to the fullest for the first time.

I Saw a Miracle

Robert (Bud) Covington was born during the great depression. Because of an alcoholic father, he was raised in an Episcopalian Boys' Home. He realized that the only way to break the chain of poverty was to get a good education, so he put himself through college and graduate school and became a geologist. He made a fortune discovering oil wells and then lost it, but he found the Gospel of Jesus Christ and he considers that the most priceless treasure of all.

My name is Robert (Bud) Covington. I came to Vernal in 1948 with the Carter Oil Company, as a geologist. I've been here ever since.

I was born in Waterloo, Iowa, March 24, 1921. When I was nine years old we moved to Chicago where my father was a journalist for the Associated Press. Times were hard in those days for this was the height of the Great Depression. My mother was working for a margarine company. She felt lucky to find a job as they were scarce. The problem was that Mother had to be on the road selling this margarine and she had three children to look out for and support. My father was an alcoholic and as a result wasn't around very much.

We were Episcopalians so Mother found a place for my brother and me in an Episcopal Boys' home. I remember being very homesick for my parents, Mother especially, when I was first sent there. I'd quietly cry myself to sleep many nights as I didn't want the other boys to think me a baby. I knew that Mother hated to put us there, but she had no other choice. There were about one hundred and fifty kids in that home. I grew up there from the time I was nine years old until I graduated from high school. It wasn't too bad. They were strict, and we had jobs to do so we learned to work. Times were tough, but we always had something to eat. They had a summer camp in Michigan. I enjoyed going there very much.

When I was about fourteen a wonderful thing happened. Mother began a job as housemother at the boys' home where we lived so I was able to be near her. We didn't have a lot but we had clothes to wear, and food to eat. I had holes in my shoes but I put cardboard in them. We went to public schools and had to walk to school which was about five miles. In the winter those five miles seemed long because of the cold. The street car went right by the home for boys where I lived and boarded, but it cost three cents to ride it, so we walked. That wind off the water of Lake Michigan can be very cold and penetrating—the coldest in the world, I sometimes thought.

I knew that my only hope of breaking this chain of poverty and helping my mother was for me to get a good education. There was no program to help young people through college then so I worked at anything I could find. I herded cows and milked them at the summer camp in upper Michigan. Then I worked at a public relations job while attending school at Loyola University. I paid for my second year at Northwestern University by cataloging the library for the observatory. By the time I was in college, the price for streetcar fare had risen to seven cents and I still couldn't afford it, so I walked and hitch-hiked ten miles to school and back every day.

The war was on so I joined the Navy and was sent to an Aviation Ordnance Bombsight School. I went aboard the U.S.S. Wasp, an aircraft carrier. We were about to ship off to sea when I received orders to go to an Officer's Training School at the University of Colorado. I finished there and was sent out to the West Coast to go overseas just as the war ended. I then went back to the University of Colorado where I received my bachelor's degree in geology. The next year I went to graduate school at the Colorado School of Mines and when I finished, I was offered a job with Carter Oil. They sent me to Vernal for my first job as a geologist.

While we lived in Chicago, my brother and I attended an Episcopal Church on Lake Shore Drive. It was a big, beautiful church, but you could sit next to the same people month after month, year after year, and you'd never know their names. They might say "Hello" or nod at you, but that was all. You never felt any warmth or that you were bonding with the people. When I arrived in Vernal I went to the Episcopal Church on Main street. I never got much out of it, but I kept going.

About seven years ago, my partner, Craig Caldwell, asked me if I'd like to go to church with him at Naples First Ward. I'd gone by that church many times but I'd never been inside. I'd seen the people go in there and come out about three or four hours later and I wondered what in the world they did in there for four hours. That seemed ridiculous! I had no idea what they did or what they believed. Then Craig asked me if I'd ever read the Book of Mormon. I answered no. He told me I should, but I never did.

I started going to church with him every Sunday. The people there were so wonderful. It was just like having a big family. My father had been gone for much of my childhood, and mother died about ten years ago. I had just one brother and one sister who both lived in other parts of the country. This ward became my new family. Everyone treated me like royalty. Their love was wonderful, but I really hadn't seen anything that converted me. I knew that these people were really close to the Lord, but I never appreciated how close.

As mentioned in the previous story, Craig and I were partners in the oil business, but had lost our money and were reduced to living on a farm in dire circumstances. I had several incidents during this time which shook me to my very foundations. The first one was when Craig and I were out in the field baling hay one hot day. We were having a hard time as the hay was too dry. Since we were so distressed financially, we needed all the hay we could get. When baling, you need a little moisture on the hay. It was almost impossible to bale that dry hay, but we'd borrowed the equipment and we needed to get the hay baled to feed our animals.

Finally Craig said, "We can't bale this dry hay. It's impossible. I'm going to say a prayer and ask the Lord for help so that we can get a little moisture." I thought to myself, Well, this is rather goofy. *There wasn't a cloud in the sky. He said a prayer and I ran to town for supplies. About fifteen minutes later, as I was coming back, I could see a small, dark cloud hovering right over where Craig was baling. It was the only cloud in the sky. I thought surely it's not going to rain right there, the only spot in the whole valley, but sure enough it rained just enough to put the moisture on the hay that we needed so desperately. Craig gratefully thanked the Lord and we continued working. I couldn't believe it! It hadn't rained anywhere else in the valley, but right over our hay, and there was just enough to moisten the hay to make it perfect to bale. This shocked me and gave me something to think about.*

As I puzzled about this miracle, I realized that Heavenly Father knew of Craig's great love for animals and their need for the hay, and he answered his sincere and humble prayer to bless them both and give me a testimony.

Whenever the home teachers came to the house, I'd always go in the other room and watch TV. I had no interest in the Church then, but after Craig received the marvelous message from the Lord that he'd never drink or smoke again, and he had quit that day and to this day has never had a drink or a smoke, I was shocked, to say the least. I knew how much he'd wanted to quit and how hard he'd tried, and this was unbelievable! Craig was accustomed to drinking a lot every night and had smoked heavily for all those many years, and all of a sudden he just quit both of those habits at once, with no bad results or withdrawal symptoms of any kind. Unbelievable! He said he'd lost all desire for liquor or cigarettes.

While he was drinking, his stomach used to bother him all the time. He continually took Tums and other medicine by the handful, but nothing helped. Now, he never took anything, nor did he seem to need it. He said the Lord cleansed his body of all impurities and detoxified it in the twinkling of an eye. I know it is true for I witnessed it.

Another incident happened that was a miracle to me. Craig got a very bad cut in his eye. It was extremely infected and painful and worried the doctor. His Salt Lake doctor was coming out from the city and would be down at Seitz Clinic that evening to see his infected eye. Craig's eye pained him dreadfully so he lay down. *When the home teachers came, he got up and talked with them and before they left they said, "You're going down to see the doctor today and we can see that you're having a dreadful problem with your eye and are really suffering. Would you like us to give you a blessing that all will be well with your eye?"*

He said, "I'd really appreciate that." They gave him a blessing and after they left he lay down. About an hour later he woke up and his eye was completely healed! We couldn't believe it! Before it had looked terribly red and inflamed. Now it was perfectly clear and all pain was gone!

He went to the doctor and after examining the eye, the doctor said, "This can't be the same eye that I was so worried about last week. This is amazing! Your eye is completely healed. What has happened since I saw you last?" Craig told him that he had a priesthood blessing that day. The doctor was impressed, to say the least. To me who knew how bad his eye was and how much it had pained him, it was really a manifestation of the power of the Lord! These things shook me up and increased my testimony, and I became really enthusiastic about going to church. I'd seen three miracles, and I knew it. After all these unbelievable things that had happened to Craig, I started listening more closely to the things that were taught there. Soon they sent the missionaries over to teach me the gospel. We went to various people's homes for the lessons. One nice thing about it was that we were always served a really good, home-cooked meal, and for two bachelors, that was great! More than that, it was the hospitality of the people—how wonderful they were! They treated us just like family.

While I was taking the lessons, I was deeply bothered by something. In our business, we'd had dealings with some people who were members of the Church and they weren't living the Christian life. To me they were hypocritical. I discussed this with the missionaries, and they said that every church has bad apples or people who do wrong, but that doesn't mean that the basic principles of the Church aren't true. I realized this is true. I had known some people in other churches who were hypocritical. I accepted that. After that I had no problem accepting the rest of the gospel.

Another thing that turned me around was the Book of Mormon. After I'd had the lessons I started reading and studying it. It dawned on me that there was no way that a young man in his early twenties with little education could ever have written the Book of Mormon without the help of the Lord. It would have been absolutely impossible. I sat down one time and tried to write two or three verses to simulate what is in the Bible and Book of Mormon and I couldn't even write two lines. I know that the Book of Mormon is true, and I know that it contains those teachings and truths that will bring us eternal life if we will live by them.

Our Bishop, Dan Olsen, called me one day and he said, "You probably know that my father, Charlie, has had a hip operation and will be home-bound for the next four or five months. He will be getting really bored. Would you mind coming by on Thursday nights and having my mother, Hazel, teach you about the Book of Mormon and other Church literature? You would also be good company for Dad." I said, "Sure," so I began to go by every Thursday evening and Sister Olsen would tell me about the historical part of the gospel. She's a wonderful teacher and I really enjoyed those lessons. One day I was reading where it said that the city of Enoch had been translated.

I said, "It says here that the city of Enoch was translated. What does translated mean?"

She said, "Taken up."

I said, "Taken up where?"

She said "Up to heaven."

I said, "Do you mean taken away from earth? What about all the people?" She said they were translated too. I never said anything but I thought to myself, I can believe most anything, but I can't believe that. It was just beyond my comprehension. I went home and I thought about that all week.

Sunday came and in the afternoon we had choir practice from four to five. I got there a little before four so I parked out in the back, north of the Church. I was the only vehicle parked back there. Everyone else was parked around by the south door. I came in the north door and went to choir practice.

After choir practice, I went down a long hall to the back door where my van was parked while the others went out the south doors. I looked and my van was not there. I thought, *Oh my word, I left the keys in my van and some kids have taken it and gone joy riding.* I was hoping that someone was still on the other side of the building so I ran around there and Bishop Haslem was just pulling out. He was the last to leave. He rolled his window down, and I said, "Someone has stolen my van. I left the keys in it and some kids must be out joy riding." He told me to get in his car and we'd drive around and see if we could find it. So I got in with him and we drove around to the back of the chapel and there, to my utter amazement, was my van. At that point I couldn't believe my eyes for there was the van and I knew that it hadn't been there five minutes before. I could see that the Bishop couldn't understand what had happened. I surely couldn't either. I thanked him and got in my van and wondered at the strange thing that I had witnessed. *Then it suddenly dawned on me that I'd just received a direct answer to my problem about translation. The Lord had shown me that being translated was not only possible. It had actually happened! I've never forgotten that experience. Whether God blinded my eyes so I couldn't see the van, or whether he'd actually removed the van from the premises for those five minutes, I don't know. I just know it was not there. Yet here it was, and I was driving it not more than five minutes after I'd searched the parking lot for it and told the Bishop that it had been stolen. I knew I'd had an answer to my prayers about the Bible and the Book of Mormon. It proved to me that all things are possible with the Lord!*

Since then I've played an active role in the Church. I taught in Primary, the High Priest class and Sunday School. Recently I was made financial clerk for the ward. I've learned how to use a computer and learned how to balance everything out. It's quite an experience!

I can truthfully say that the Book of Mormon is true. Joseph Smith was a true prophet, as Gordon B. Hinckley is a true prophet today. Christ looks with favor upon The Church of Jesus Christ of Latter-day Saints and blesses it. It's His Church and He is the head of it. I am so grateful for this knowledge. It has changed my life completely.

Rescued by a Dream

I read this amazing story in the Deseret News in 1947 and it so intrigued me that I've kept a copy of it all these years. When I started this book I wanted to include this story. I tried to contact George Hunt, the man who had the dream, but found he had passed on. Finally I found his son, who shared with me the following account his father had written shortly after the miraculous rescue of Dr. and Mrs. Robert Dykes.

November 8, 1947, was a cold fall day at the ranch ten miles northwest of Roosevelt, Utah where I farmed and raised livestock. On the evening news it was reported that a California doctor, H. Robert Dykes, and his wife were missing on a flight from Custer, South Dakota, (via Rawlings, Wyoming), to Salt Lake City, Utah.

I had been taking flight instructions for a few months. A few weeks before, I had attempted to fly my first cross-country flight, so I took a great interest in this news and kept current with all the broadcasts about the lost plane. There were many planes searching for the missing couple, but no trace of the plane or people had been found.

The evening of November 11, I took the one air chart I had, SALT LAKE CITY (U-3), and spread it out on the kitchen table to study it. This chart covered the Uintah Mountains, including King's Peak at 13,498 feet and Gilbert Peak at 13,422 feet.

Years before I had ridden over the horse trail from the head of King's and Gilbert peaks. At the top of this pass, over 12,000 feet elevation, I had stood and looked with awe at the unbelievable beauty of the panorama below. As I studied this chart and thought of the rough area where the plane might have crashed, I felt sick inside. The couple had a very slim chance of survival after four days of being lost.

I listened to the ten o'clock news, but there was no news of the missing plane. *I went to bed with this on my mind and, after saying a prayer for the people who were possibly injured, somewhere in the cold, I lay awake for what seemed like hours. I simply couldn't get them off my mind. When I finally slept, I had a dream. In my dream I saw a snow-covered ridge, and I could see a downed plane and two people waving and calling for help. The dream was so vivid that it startled me and I woke up. I felt I should know this place where they were, for it looked vaguely familiar. When I finally drifted off to sleep, the same dream occurred again. This time I was viewing the scene from a distance. I could still see the plane in the snow and the people waving for help. I awoke with a start, got out of bed and went to the kitchen table where I had left the spread-out air chart.*

As I again studied the chart, my attention focused on the peaks I was most acquainted with. As a young boy in my teens, I had fished most of the lakes in those High Uintah mountains with my friends, riding our horses from one lake to another. *I soon went back to bed and finally fell into a troubled sleep. Again I had the same dream or vision. This time I could still see the peaks in the background and the plane, but in the foreground was a big grassy meadow with rolling knolls. It came to me in a flash. It was Painter's Basin, with King's Peak and Gilbert Peak in the background. It was daylight when I woke again. I had to do something about this dream, but what or how?*

While I was milking cows and doing my farm chores, *I could not stop thinking about those people and my dream.* I could think of nothing else although I tried to ignore it. It was as if some unseen force was urging me on.

I was a student pilot and had just 20 hours 55 minutes solo flying time built up over the past fourteen months. I felt I was progressing well, but I knew my instructor, Joe Mower, didn't have much faith in my flying ability, and he didn't keep his feelings secret from me either. I knew if I went to Joe and told him I'd had a dream in which I'd found the Dykes, he and the others would laugh me right out of the hanger.

Besides, he wouldn't let me take the plane outside the ten-mile limit he'd set for me.

Then I thought of Hal Crumbo, a Ute Indian, who went with me on my first cross-country flight. I'd met Hal for the first time on this flight and liked him. He'd done a great deal of flying in World War II, and his advice would be helpful. I knew that if I could get Hal off to the side and tell him of my dreams he would be willing to help.

After my chores were finished, I went in for breakfast. While eating I listened to the news on the radio. I felt sick when it said that the search for the Dykes had been called off and the plane wouldn't be found until spring.

I could think of nothing else but my irrepressible urge to find the plane. I knew full well the danger involved, so I tried to talk myself out of doing such a foolhardy thing. I knew that if a larger plane with an experienced pilot couldn't make it in those high mountains, I didn't have much chance. *I also knew that if I searched for the plane in the area I'd been shown in my dream that I'd surely find it. I knew my dream was from the Lord—a cry for help from those people, and probably an answer to prayers. I was meant to rescue them. I knew that I couldn't live with myself if I didn't try.*

I went to the airport. Hal wasn't there and Joe, the instructor, was in town picking up the mail. A teen-aged boy had been left in charge. An unseen force seemed to be pushing me on. I asked to fly the Aeronica NC85637 and the boy and I pushed the plane out of the hanger. I got in and he propped it up, and then he came to the window and asked me where I was going. I said, "To look for the Dykes," and gave it the throttle. I was on my way but I was going against the rules. I felt bad about that, but it seemed a small thing in comparison to saving the lives of those stranded people.

I put the plane into a steady climb and headed for King's Peak. When I reached Uintah Canyon I realized I didn't know what I was doing. I'd never flown over mountains like these. I flew to the West over Crebe's Basin, into Chain Lakes Basin and over the Atwood Lake Basin. At the base of Mt. Emmons Peak, at 13,428 feet, I searched the saddles and passes north of King's Peak. As I turned east to Gilbert Peak, I was beginning to wonder if my dreams had any real meaning.

Maybe they were just dreams after all. I'd been sure I'd find the plane somewhere between King's Peak and Gilbert Peak but it wasn't there. The high winds, downdrafts, and rough air were giving me trouble in the little 65 horse-power plane. I was losing altitude and had to pull back from the peaks, but I kept flying near them.

I felt very disappointed about not finding the plane where I was sure it was, but I didn't have much time to think about that for I realized that although I had the throttle all the way in I was going down fast. Somehow I pulled out of the downdraft and continued on to the north. The wind was fierce. The downdrafts and rough air continued to give me trouble in the small plane, but somehow, in spite of my great fear, I couldn't give up looking even though I knew that at any moment I might hit a mighty downdraft that would throw me to the bottom of the canyon to my death.

I found that I had searched all over the mountain except for Burro's Peak, about ten miles to the east of Gilbert Peak. I simply couldn't stop until I'd searched there. Some unseen force, greater than the fear, seemed to spur me on.

Burro's Peak finally came into view. Maybe my dream was "just a dream" after all, I chided myself, as I viewed the vast, white blank expanse before me. I searched fervently, but there was nothing. I've made this dangerous trip and risked my life for nothing, I thought bitterly, as I turned my plane toward the north. I'll go home now. Just then out of the corner of my eye, I caught a flash of something. My heart pounded as I turned to get a better look. Then I had the thrill of a lifetime! *I'd spotted the downed plane just as in my dreams! Both people were waving furiously, one with a big coat and the other with a blanket just like the people in my dreams!* I opened the window and waved at them. I wigwagged my wings to let them know I saw them, but the wind was tossing me around and I doubt if they saw my wigwags.

"Thank you, God, thank you, God!" I cried. "Thank you for letting me play a part in saving the lives of these people." Such joy and relief filled my heart as I'd never known. I cried like a baby. After twenty-seven years, I still cannot tell this story without crying. Now my only thought was to get out of there and back to the airport so I could report the found plane and get help for those people.

I knew I was in serious trouble as I headed for the Uintah Canyon, for I was still in a downdraft and unable to gain altitude. When I reached timberline at 11,000 feet, I was right down to the tree tops and *I was saying a prayer to the Lord for help. Suddenly I recalled an article I'd read in a flying magazine a week or so before. It was on mountain flying about downdrafts and updrafts. If the writer knew what he was talking about, there should be an updraft at the east side of Uintah Canyon.* I needed something desperately to help me gain altitude and get over the mountain. I started to move over near the canyon wall. I put the left wing as near the canyon wall as I dared. Then I hit an updraft with such force that I was literally lifted out of the canyon. *I said a fervent prayer of thanksgiving.* I knew that I'd hit the updraft just in time, for the small plane couldn't gain altitude in the downdraft. I flew to the airport as quickly as possible. I'd been gone an hour and thirty minutes. When I taxied up and cut the motor, Joe was there to meet me breathing fire. "You're grounded," he screamed. Then he started cursing me for being an idiot and breaking the ten-mile limit without an instructor.

"Joe, I know I broke the rules and I'm sorry, but I found the Dykes and they need help. Let's get it to them as quickly as we can."

I headed for the hanger and the phone. Joe never let up on me. He just knew I was lying. The idea that I'd found that plane in an hour and a half when dozens of planes had searched for it for a week was ludicrous.

I walked right to the phone and asked for the operator. When she answered, I said, "I want the Civil Air Patrol in Salt Lake City." When they came on the phone I asked if any trace of the Dykes plane had been found. She said that there was no chance of them being alive and that the search had been called off until spring. I informed her that they had been found and were both alive, and that we were going to drop food and supplies to them as soon as possible. Joe had stopped chewing on me and was standing there with his mouth open.

Everyone got busy. Joe and I went to town to get food and blankets. Someone called Hal Crumbo and Howard Dennis. There was great excitement as the news was broadcast that the Dykes had been found alive.

When Joe and I returned with the supplies, we were told that the phone had been ringing off the wall. Everyone wanted to know the location of the plane. I told them it was east of Gilbert Peak in the Uintahs.

Hal had his Stearman (bi-plane) loaded with the supplies. I was to lead Hal and his helper to the downed plane. I certainly wasn't grounded this time.

Again I was on my way back up to the high peaks. Hal's plane was larger and faster than the Aeronica I was in, so he was flying out ahead and above me. When I got up to Painter's Basin at 11,000 feet, I met the downdrafts again and was right in the treetops. I could see Hal circling above and ahead of me and I knew he was in range of the downed plane. I could not get any higher so I just had to hope they would spot it. I didn't have to wait long. Hal came out of his circle and headed for the plane. I figured I had done all I could. Now I was in big trouble again. The same wind was blowing, so I used the same procedure, searching for the updraft, and thankfully, found it and was lifted from the canyon again.

When I returned to the airport, Howard Dennis grabbed me. He said that everyone was going wild to get the exact longitude and latitude of the plane. Between us we figured out the required information.

I started calling men with horses. We also needed a truck to haul them to the U Bar Ranch which was the closest place to the crash. I finally got the ground rescue crew rounded up. There were Harold Loranger and Clifford Woodward, each with his own horse.

I was leaving for my ranch to get my horse when Hal landed. He was surprised to see me alive. He'd spent an hour or so looking for my plane. After they'd dropped the supplies to the Dykes, they turned and I'd disappeared. He just knew that there was no way I could have gotten out of that canyon in that 65 HP plane as he was having difficulty with a 250 HP plane. He told Joe that if I could get that small Aeronica in and out of there twice with the fierce wind blowing like it was, he didn't have to worry about me flying anywhere.

It was getting dark as the three of us in the rescue party left my ranch. Arben Wilkerson let us take his old truck. Three of us climbed into the cab of the truck. It was crowded, but it was too cold to ride back with the horses. That ride through the snow-filled road to the empty ranch house, and the night we spent there on the cold floor with just a thin blanket, each are memories I'd as soon forget as there was no wood to make a fire and it was bitter cold.

We got up when the moon came up, for we knew we must cross a dangerous shale dugway later which was treacherous even in summer. We reached the dugway about daylight. We were leading our horses, as the trail had been obliterated by snow. Suddenly Cliff's horse, Buck, fell head over heels down to the ice of the Duchesne River below. Not only did we lose her, but all the food we had was tied to Buck's saddle.

Climbing up that steep mountain in the snow, and trying to make it over that shale dugway where the rocks were so loose and treacherous was one of the hardest and most hazardous tasks I'd undertaken except for the plane ride in search of the Dykes. *We had a prayer in our hearts all that way.* How happy we were when we got over the dugway!

As we came over the ridge, we saw the plane about a half mile away. What a thrill it was to see the Dykes standing there waving! Now our goal was in sight. We knew our horses couldn't make it over the rocks ahead, so we tied them up and started running. We forgot about being hungry, cold and tired, we were so happy to see them! All those many hours of suspense and the ordeal we'd been through for so long in the cold was forgotten. As we approached the scene, we could see men from the Wyoming side coming into view. Several planes were flying overhead also. It was a time of rejoicing for everyone!

The thing that both pleased and surprised our rescue party was the fact that Mrs. Dykes had a pot of hot soup and a pot of hot coffee waiting for us. We'd thought our next meal was down a dangerous mountain trail, and some twenty miles of snowbound road and at least twenty hours away. After a bowl or two of hot soup and a couple of cups of coffee, things looked a lot better to our group. Never had warm food tasted so delicious as it did to three half-frozen men!

It was soon decided to take the Dykes down the Wyoming side of the mountain. The trail was shorter and much safer. They also had two horses at the scene for them to ride on. I've often thought that they might not have lived if we'd taken them down with us, so hazardous was our trail.

Dr. Dykes told us how he took the settling bulb of the oil system and placed it on the cabin floor where gas would drop in it. After he had the gas regulated to a steady drip, he lighted it. With a map over the hole in the windshield where his head had stuck through in the crash, they were able to have a little warmth, although the smoke was awful. They'd run out of gas the morning I found them.

I talked with Mrs. Dykes while we were eating lunch. She also told me some of the things they did to survive. "We sucked on icicles and *prayed all the time.*" She said they thought they had a chance of being rescued until they heard on their radio that the search had been called off until spring. They knew they could not live through another freezing night without food or blankets to keep them warm. "We were in the depths of despair then."

After they were packed up and on their way, the three of us ran as fast as we could to our horses. If there was any way possible, we knew we must get across the shale dugway before it got completely dark. Our very lives depended on it! When we reached our horses, we felt sorry for them. They looked so gaunt and cold. They'd had nothing to eat or drink but the snow they'd eaten.

We trotted and galloped whenever we could and took turns running. The sun had gone down and it was dusk as we neared the bridge. We wondered if Buck had died in her fall, but then we heard her whinny so we knew that she was still alive. Was she happy to see us! We turned her loose and gave her a chance to follow us. We had to get across that dugway while there was still a speck of daylight left. As we rode away, she started trying to shuffle her feet and move a little. We knew she'd follow if she could move at all. We crossed the dugway without mishap and after what seemed like ages, we came to the truck.

A prayer was in my heart. "Now, dear God please let this cold, old truck start." The battery would hardly turn the motor over. We were all praying silently because so much depended on that cold motor. Just about the time we'd given up on the truck, the motor started. What sweet music to our ears! I turned on the lights and we wasted no time getting the horses loaded. Even with three of us crowded in the cab, we were happy when the heater started warming us up.

It was morning by the time we arrived back at the ranch. Men and horses were completely exhausted, but we all felt great satisfaction! We had put forth our best efforts for our fellow men! *Best of all, my faith in prayer had been renewed. I knew without a doubt that the Lord lives and answers prayers, for He had led me to find the Dykes and help rescue them!*

The Rest of the Story

Twenty-seven years later, Mrs. Dykes, now Mrs. Stewart, had a reunion with me. *She said she'd prayed all night the night before I found them. While she was praying, I'd been having the three dreams of their downed plane, the familiar mountain peaks and them waving to me.* She told of hearing over the radio that the search had been called off and the utter despair they felt. It was then that they'd written the letters to their children telling them what they hoped they would do with their lives in case they were destined never to return to them.

Mrs. Stewart said, "Seeing the little red and yellow plane and you waving to us was the most beautiful sight we'd ever seen, and the happiest moment of our lives! When you didn't circle back, I was afraid I'd imagined that you'd waved, but we were reassured when within two hours, the Roosevelt Flying Service dropped blankets, food and a note telling us that help was on the way.

"No one can even imagine our heart-felt gratitude to you for saving our lives! I know that God lives and answers prayers, for how do you explain your dreams that drove you to risk your life for people you didn't even know, while I was praying fervently and desperately for help. I owe my life to you, George Hunt, for listening to the Lord's urging and saving our lives!"

God Kept His Promise

While visiting our daughter, Julie, and her husband, Dr. Peter Carruth, in Crailsheim, Germany in 1970, we heard this dynamic testimony from a Regional Representative during Sacrament Meeting. It so deeply impressed me that I recorded it in my journal twenty-eight years ago. Here is his story.

We were stationed in Florida, many years ago. I had just finished lunch one hot day when the doorbell rang. My wife, Gloria, went to the door and soon came back saying that two Mormon missionaries were at the door. I said, "I'll soon get rid of them." I went to the door with a cigarette in one hand and a can of beer in the other with the full intention of asking them to leave, but something about those clean-cut young boys touched me in some strange way, so instead, I asked them in. They said they represented The Church of Jesus Christ of Latter-day Saints and told us a little about their church and then asked if we would care to have the missionary lessons. Frankly, I didn't want to hear any more. I was perfectly comfortable with my lifestyle and knew if I accepted this church, I'd have to change in some way. Gloria, on the other hand, wanted to know more about the Mormon Church and was in favor of having the lessons, so she asked the young men to return. They left a Book of Mormon and promised to return in a couple of days.

Out of curiosity, I started to read the book, thinking this was just another foolish, man-made religion. To my amazement, I became enthralled with the book. My wife also began to read it during the day while I was gone, and she said that she couldn't tear herself away from it. I feared that it was true and I didn't want to believe it. That would necessitate a change and commitment in my life that I felt unable and unwilling to make at that time.

When the missionaries returned to give the lessons, I purposely planned to have another appointment, so I was absent. My wife and children had the first discussion and when I returned, that was all they could talk about. They were thrilled and insisted that I attend the next one, but I had other plans. I simply didn't want to get involved and missed several discussions on purpose.

One evening the doorbell rang. It was the missionaries. One of them, Elder Blake, said that they were in the neighborhood and their appointment wasn't home. They wondered if they might give us another of the discussions that evening even though it was a day earlier than their appointment. Of course, Gloria was delighted. "I'm so happy that you came. Bob is home tonight," she said.

As we listened to the discussions, I had a strange feeling that this gospel wasn't new to me, and that I'd heard it somewhere before. It all rang true and seemed familiar. Gloria was so full of questions that the missionaries stayed several hours. When they left, they said they'd keep their appointment with us for the next evening.

I felt that I really wanted to hear more of the discussions so I was present. It was then that one of the young men told us of the Word of Wisdom and the fact that their church didn't believe in smoking or drinking. They knew I smoked and drank beer for they'd seen me the first day we met. What they didn't know was just how hooked I was on cigarettes and that I was also an alcoholic. I had never admitted that even to myself until I thought of giving it up. How could I? I was around men who drank and smoked continually. Also, our social life revolved around having a drink with friends. All the people we knew and all our friends drank and smoked. Not only that, but I now felt I needed a drink and often drank alone. I was in a quandary, for I was anxious to hear more of the Church, but I knew that I couldn't live its precepts, even if it was true. I refused to attend more of the discussions.

After taking the lessons, Gloria accepted the gospel as did the children, but I couldn't bring myself to, even though I knew it was true. I didn't think I was capable of changing my life so completely.

She and the children started going to church and living the gospel, and what a change it made in their lives! *The missionaries were present a great deal in our home, and I could feel the sweet spirit of the Lord when they were there.*

Gloria and I began drifting apart. She no longer wanted to go to the Officer's Club when I went. I often came home late at night smelling of liquor and cigarette smoke, and when I did, she looked hurt. I fought the adversary night and day. I knew that Gloria wanted me to join the Church, although she didn't pressure me. I also knew that it was the best thing that had ever happened to our children, but I couldn't quite bring myself to give up my old life and the ingrained habits of many years, and commit myself to the Church with its strict beliefs about cigarettes, liquor, and morality.

One night I came home from the club rather late. I was intoxicated and smelled strongly of cigarette smoke. Gloria was still up waiting for me and I could see the hurt in her eyes. *I went to bed and must have dozed off, for I had a dream. My eyes seemed to be open as never before to the kind of person I'd become. A panorama of my life seemed to unfold as if on a movie screen. I saw everything I'd done. I'd cheated on my wife and had lived a godless life. What I saw almost made me ill, for I knew I was a wicked man. I felt Gloria's disappointment in me and her withdrawal. I saw myself continuing on the path I was on and losing my wife and family and saw the loneliness and heartache I would suffer. I remembered that in Mosiah it said that the natural man is an enemy to God and always will be unless he yields to the enticings of the Holy Spirit. I realized that Mosiah was talking about me. Suddenly, the scene changed and I could see what would happen in my life if I truly repented and accepted the gospel. I saw myself having the strength to break my addictions with the Lord's help. A great happiness filled my heart. I saw what joy I would give Gloria and the children if I would join, and how it would change our children's lives to have their father as a worthy example.*

When I awoke, I knew what I must do. I must join the Church! I'd really known it was true right from the first time I started to read the Book of Mormon. I repented of every wrong I'd ever done, and asked the Lord's forgiveness. I had a struggle with my addictions, but with the

Lord's help, I finally quit my bad habits. How grateful I was to be free of those vices that had made a slave of me.

It was a great day when I was baptized and joined The Church of Jesus Christ of Latter-day Saints. A peace came into my heart that I'd never known, and the happiness it brought my family was marvelous to see.

I was soon called to leave for overseas. My job was to pilot a helicopter which flew right into the front lines to pick up the wounded and dead. Our helicopters were unarmed so we were "sitting ducks" as targets. We probably had the most dangerous job in the Air Force.

My unit was stationed in Hawaii, and we had orders to leave the next day for the front. I felt a deep depression settle over me. I just knew I would never return alive. Some of the fellows were going out to party one last time. We all knew that many of us would not come back alive. Although they knew that I'd stopped going out with them, the fellows urged me to go, saying that this would be our last chance to have fun for a long time and maybe forever. Satan really tempted me to go with them. What did it matter, I asked myself. I knew that many of us would soon be dead and I'd be among them. That would be the end.

Even though I didn't feel like praying in that black mood that threatened to overcome me, I sat on my bunk and prayed silently for strength to resist temptation and have guidance in my life. *Suddenly I knew where I wanted to go that night, and that was to the temple. It was not too far away, and even though Satan kept telling me that it was useless to go, I went regardless. After the session, the temple president, whom I didn't know, came to me and said, "Brother, I have a strong feeling that you need a special blessing tonight." I was shocked and surprised. I felt that if anyone ever needed a blessing I was that person so I welcomed the blessing wholeheartedly. I wondered how he knew of the temptations I'd had and the deep depression I felt.*

The president took me into his private chambers, and I've never heard such a marvelous blessing or felt the Spirit of the Lord so powerfully in my life. Among other great predictions about my future, the president told me that if I would keep my covenants, I would come home to my family unharmed and find them well and eagerly awaiting my return.

I had entered the temple full of doubts and fears; I left with calm assurance that I would not be harmed. How thankful I was that I hadn't given in to temptation and gone out with the men during that dark hour when Satan was tempting me. Instead, I'd come to the temple and received this marvelous blessing!

During the next few months, I flew many missions through enemy gunfire to pick up the dead and the wounded. Over two-thirds of our helicopters were destroyed, and many of my comrades lost their lives. *The Lord blessed me, for I was totally without fear. I knew if I kept my part of the bargain, God would keep His part and I'd be safe.* Finally, my commander was determined to take me off such dangerous missions and give me leave since I'd more than fulfilled my assignment. Although he urged me to be relieved of such dangerous duty, I asked to stay longer. Many of my comrades were extremely fearful of flying those unarmed helicopters right into the midst of battle. They had a right to be frightened, for they saw many of their friends die or be maimed each day. I knew I was protected, and I thought I might save some of my friends' lives if I took their place. I was willing to stay as long as my commanding officer would let me.

Brother Rice did stay longer than necessary, flying into the heaviest gunfire to rescue comrades. He won the highest honors possible including the Purple Heart. Of this he said, "It wasn't because I was brave, but because of that great blessing I'd been given in the temple that night. I knew with a certainty that if I was faithful, I would return to my family unharmed." Finally, when the war was over, he returned home to his family whole and healthy, and they were joyfully awaiting his return!

Most Likely to Succeed

Dr. Frank Wilson is a prominent surgeon and respected member of his community. He is also frank in admitting that he is a former drug addict. He spends time talking with school students about the evils of alcohol and drugs and gives three months each year as a member of a team of doctors who travel to third world countries and give their time and expertise freely to help those in need. This is his story.

As I look at my high school yearbook, I feel it is ironic that the words, "Most Likely to Succeed," are under my picture. I now realize that I had the opportunity and the qualifications to succeed, and I nearly threw it all away due to an almost overpowering drug habit.

I was born of good, religious parents, one of nine boys. Father developed many health problems while trying to get his degree. Doctors said it was mainly from stress and that he must leave school for a time and get out in the open, so our family moved to a small community and Dad was made Superintendent of Schools there, a job he could easily handle without too many problems. Dad was eventually called back to Provo to head a pilot program of the seminary. We children were thankful, for we loved Provo.

School was always easy for me, and while I was attending BYU, I decided to become a doctor although how I was to get the money to send myself through school, I didn't know. I surely couldn't expect my parents to put me through since they had so many children and boys on missions. This was before the time of student loans.

I won a partial scholarship from the Y which would help me, but I knew that I'd have to work the rest of my way through school. The problem was that working plus the load in medical school was considered too difficult for any student, and was frowned upon by the school. It seemed that many who had tried it had breakdowns of one kind or another.

I was accepted at Northwestern University in Chicago, got settled in the least-expensive quarters I could find, and started looking for a job with hours that wouldn't conflict with my schooling. The only job that I could find was working in an emergency hospital at night. I'd have my days free for school. That would mean that I'd get very little sleep, but I felt I could manage it.

I was excited about school. In fact, I loved it, but the job was something else. It left little time for sleep. We called Saturday night "Knife and Gun Club Night." There were so many knifings and shootings, I was often up all night. I was totally exhausted and had a hard time keeping awake in class. However, I studied hard and did well.

We were due for the final exam for the semester one day, and I'd had a particularly stressful night at the hospital with absolutely no sleep. I was at the point of complete exhaustion and didn't know how I was going to stay awake long enough to get through the exam. Then the thought suddenly struck me that drugs were available and if I could only take something for this one final exam, I could get through it and no one would be the wiser. I talked myself into taking one amphetamine against my better judgment and all I'd been taught.

The results were extraordinary and exhilarating. I was wide awake and my mind perfectly clear during the exam. That awful weariness that I'd been experiencing was completely gone and I breezed through the test with ease and a great grade. How grateful I was for that little pill. I didn't know that I'd pay later and at a much larger price than I'd anticipated.

After using once, it's easier to do it again. I now knew what effect the pill would have, and so the next time I was completely fatigued, I took a pill. Soon it took two pills to pep me up, and whenever a test was coming up I took a couple more. In order to maintain my brutal work pace, two pills didn't work any more. Soon I was taking more and more amphetamines every morning. I didn't think of being hooked, only of surviving during this difficult time of little sleep and an enormous work load. The use of stimulants hardly seemed to me to be cause for alarm. I'd come quite a way down the road since I'd taken my first pill with such a guilty conscience. Of course, I thought no one knew but me. The use of stimulants made me talk a little faster, but people at the hospital had never known me when I was drug free and I didn't think anyone detected it at school. I didn't think that serious physical addiction to amphetamines was possible, so I didn't worry about periodically boosting the dosage to maintain the extra-energy effect required to keep me going.

The fellows I lived with loved to gamble but I stayed away from their games. For one thing, it was against my religion, and for another, I didn't have money to gamble with, but one day they dared me to join them in a game. "We won't play for money if you'll play this once," they said.

I got in on the game and won easily. I kept thinking that if I'd played for money, I would have made quite a sum. The next time they played they asked me to play, and I told them no. I frankly told them that I couldn't afford to play. They promised to play for very low stakes. As luck would have it, I won again. It wasn't much money—but just enough to whet my appetite for more. What I didn't realize was that they were letting me win so I'd play with them.

Little by little, I was drawn into their games. It was a form of relaxation that I enjoyed until one day I lost heavily. The guys said I could pay them when I could. I felt awful, but when the next game came around, I felt I had to participate in order to win and pay back my debt. I won a little and paid back some of the money I owed. "See how easy it is," Jack, one of the fellows said. "Some days you win and some days you lose. It about evens up."

I had always been a church-goer, but I found that now I had little time or inclination to go to church. My conscience hurt me about the pills and gambling, but I didn't want to stop while I was deprived of sleep and until my schooling was over. I kept telling myself that as soon as I graduated, I'd never touch a pill again, and I would stop gambling and become active in my church.

As I advanced in school, the pressure and intensity of the studies increased. I was still working at the emergency hospital, and I felt I'd learned a great deal there, but it also had taken a toll on me. Now I was using larger and larger doses of amphetamines, not only through the exams, but every day. "It's only until I'm through medical school," I kept telling myself. I felt that I could quit any time. By now, my morning intake had jumped considerably. I simply couldn't continue my studies without the lift those drugs gave me. As time progressed, I took more and more amphetamines until by my senior year, I was using more heavily than I dared to think.

I often wonder how I kept up with my studies, but I had fairly high grades considering the hours of work I put in at the hospital and the little time I had for studying. My teachers were impressed at my skill in surgery and complimented me highly. I was told many times that I was missing my calling if I didn't take another two years and major in it. I would have loved to continue my studies, but I felt that if I lasted long enough to graduate as a doctor, I'd be lucky. Finally, I received my diploma. How happy and relieved I was to know that I would never have to work in the emergency hospital again, and that I could have a good night's sleep once in awhile.

I returned to Salt Lake to intern at the LDS Hospital. During the depression, interns received very small wages, so I continued to gamble and won more often than I lost for I'd learned to play well by that time. I swore to myself that I was through with drugs, but now I had a craving for them that I couldn't control.

One day I ran into a beautiful girl I'd known at the Y. Her name was Carmen Crane and she now was living in Salt Lake and employed as an airline stewardess. Those were the days when an airline stewardess had to be a trained nurse, and Carmen had just recently graduated from nurse's training. She was the only child of a professor at the Y and the loveliest girl I'd ever met. She had a beautiful face, black, curly hair and bright blue eyes! I fell deeply in love with her and she with me. We were married, even though I was still working as an intern and making practically nothing. She made enough to rent a small apartment so that we could be together when possible. With her strange hours and mine, that time was limited. We both looked forward to the time when I'd be through my internship and I could settle into a practice.

I'd never told Carmen about my drug habit and was striving to quit it, but my hours were long at the hospital. Even though I was trying to stop, it seemed impossible for now I needed that extra boost drugs gave me.

Great was our rejoicing when I finished my internship. I was now ready to practice on my own. We went to Provo, and I opened my practice, but people didn't flock to me as I'd anticipated as there were so many doctors in that area. To make matters more complicated, Carmen was now expecting our first child and unable to work. Somehow we scraped by, but we had to borrow money to run the office and we were deep in debt. Drugs were my means of escape. When I was high, I didn't worry about the debts and so I continued to use.

When our first child, a beautiful little girl, Judith, was born, we should have been happy, but there was always the specter of unpaid bills and little money to haunt us.

By a lucky coincidence, I was offered a position in a clinic in a small, isolated town in Wyoming. We were overjoyed and immediately moved there for we were sure of a fairly good income. Carmen was now expecting our second child. I loved the work at the small clinic-hospital. I did most of the operating and that was the field I loved.

We bought a nice home, paid some of our bills, and I was soon seeing up to thirty patients a day, plus operating a couple of days a week. I was not sleeping well so I decided to moonlight to bring my salary up high enough to be able to pay all my bills in a couple of years. The only problem was that my intake of amphetamines was now very high. However, I didn't like the idea of using drugs while operating so I vowed to quit.

I decided it was imperative that I kick the drug habit once and for all. During a week's vacation I stopped all drugs. Almost immediately my energy level fell to zero. I became cross, grouchy and depressed. When my children wanted to go swimming, I told them I was sleepy; when Carmen wanted to see a movie, I told her I didn't feel well.

Two days off stimulants and I was a nervous wreck, so I started taking an oral narcotic—one tablet three times a day—to get by. I became a pleasant person again. The rest of the vacation went nicely without amphetamines. I figured I'd take the narcotic for a week or so until my energy returned, but I enjoyed the effect so much that I just kept taking it. I also missed my amphetamine regimen so I started it again.

We added on to the small clinic and this wing was mainly for surgery. Since I did most of the surgery, and was either in surgery or with patients, I was no longer working closely with the other doctors. There was no one to question my behavior, which was becoming more and more erratic. I knew that it was becoming uncontrollable, yet I was powerless to change.

Now I needed narcotics. The prescription I wrote for a large amount of tablets lasted about a month. The exhilarating "rush" began to fade. I stepped up the dosage, one every four hours. I knew that was a lot, but now I needed it. Soon that wasn't enough, so I started taking one every three hours, and then one every two hours—until I couldn't get a buzz off a tablet an hour. The only solution I had was to take more. I felt like a drowning man grasping for a straw. I became irritable and began to have a difficult time controlling my temper. I was afraid I'd lose my composure in front of the patients for I had no patience with their constant talk about their ills.

Soon it became difficult for me to keep food down and my stomach pain became terrifying. Antacids didn't do anything for the pain. I finally resorted to taking a powerful painkiller and sedatives. An injection of that eradicated my stomach pain and made me sleep. My drug use was interfering with my practice of surgery and I knew it, but I seemed helpless to stop.

Finally I told my wife the dilemma I was in and that I wanted to quit. She was deeply shaken and shocked by the depth of my drug use, but promised to help me fight it. We sent the children to be with her sister for awhile. I knew enough from medical school that withdrawal from the drugs could be accomplished if done right. By keeping myself sedated for about 3 days, I could shake my addiction and be drug free. My faithful wife stayed at my bedside day and night, taking my blood pressure and pulse and occasionally awakening me to see if I was all right.

I returned to work free of drugs a week later, but I was so keyed up that I couldn't get any sleep or relax in any way. I fought my addiction like a demon, but it now had me in its clutches to the point that two weeks later, I was back on amphetamines. Four weeks later my daily dose had climbed so high it was frightening.

By summer I was also taking a large dose of a narcotic nightly in order to get some sleep. I found that I needed more and more until I began shooting up each morning. Soon that wasn't enough so I'd shoot up every few hours during the day. I'd feel a wonderful surge of pleasure as the narcotic entered my bloodstream, but only temporarily for soon I craved it again. Now nothing mattered but getting my "fix." I found it hard to be civil to patients if they started to ramble.

I remembered that when I had been interning and seeing addicts, it seemed clear to me that my patients were disgustingly weak-willed people. Why did they do it, I often wondered. Surely it would be easy to break a drug habit with a little self-control. I made heroic efforts to quit, but when I was tired or depressed, my willpower would erode and I'd be back on them. I often thought of that first pill I'd taken and wished with all my heart that I'd never started.

We had two fine, healthy children, business was thriving and I should have been happy and I would have been but for the "monkey on my back." How I prayed that I'd be able to master this terrible habit that was haunting me day and night.

Although Carmen had helped me get off drugs once, I knew that she suspected that I was on them again. She knew something was terribly wrong from my mood swings. This was causing a rift between us.

One Saturday I was tired and depressed by the way our marriage was going and sick about the drug habit which I seemed helpless to quit. It was my weekend off and so I got really stoned. I was lying in a hammock on the patio, oblivious to the world around me when my wife awakened me. "Heidi is on the phone. She said there is an emergency and Dr. Hudson called in sick. Will you take it?"

Heidi was the nurse on duty that day. In my hazy condition I knew that it would be impossible for me to take care of an emergency. "I can't," I told Carmen. "Call Dr. Hudson and see if he can't come regardless or get someone else. It's his case." There was no other hospital in our small town and no hospital nearby to send the emergency to.

Carmen phoned Dr. Hudson's home, only to find that he'd been running a high fever and was extremely ill.

"You've got to go," Carmen said. "You're the only doctor who can operate and the nurse says the patient needs surgery now. Get up and get ready."

I struggled to my feet and swayed into the house. Everything was spinning around so fast that I had a hard time walking. Carmen followed me in. "You're drunk," Carmen said scornfully. "I've known for a long time that you've been either drinking or on drugs again. Now a person's life is at stake and you're in no condition to help."

"I will, I must," I said. My tongue was so thick that I could hardly speak. I'd really overdone it with the drugs this time. *"Oh, God, please help me," I cried silently.*

Carmen helped me into the shower. Then I got into my clothes. "I'd better take you to the clinic," Carmen said. "You're in no condition to drive."

I held onto her arm while we walked into the hospital and to the emergency room. The man on the operating table was holding his side and moaning. Even in my hazy state of mind, I could tell he probably had appendicitis and needed an operation immediately. I knew that it was up to me.

As I washed up for the operation, I kept asking God to help me. Never in my life had I felt so humble or so dependent on Him. I knew that without His help, I simply couldn't get through the operation.

The nurse gave the patient anesthetic and I splashed cold water on my face and waited for the anesthetic to take effect. All the time I was silently pleading with God to help me, and promising Him that if He would guide my hand this once, I would get help, kick the habit forever, and change my life.

As I took the knife into my hand, a calm settled on me. My mind cleared, and my hand was steady. I knew that the Lord was indeed helping me, for I performed a perfect operation that day. I might also add that it was the last I would perform for over a year, for that night I met with my colleagues from the clinic. I told them that I was addicted to drugs, that the addiction had come on me while I was in medical school and working nights at the emergency hospital, and that I'd be leaving to start treatment. "Find another doctor to take my place. I don't know how long my treatment will take. I'm sorry I let you down." They told me that they wanted me back and would hold my place until I returned. Their confidence in me brought tears to my eyes. How grateful I was for such friends.

As I was dropped off the next day at the drug detoxification clinic in a large city, I was ashamed and frightened. My self-esteem was at its lowest, but worst of all, despite all the love and support I'd received from my family, I felt alone. My wife said they had a new treatment which was proving very successful. During the first few days, I was detoxified with the help of tranquilizers. Then I was assigned to an apartment with other addicts and alcoholics, half of whom were physicians. Suddenly, I didn't feel so alone. Most of the physicians and psychologists who examined me were also recovering addicts. I began to feel like a person and not an addict.

When the treatment was over, even the thought of drugs made me nauseous and still does. I have kept my promise to the Lord and have never touched any kind of drug since that fateful day when I could feel Him guiding my hand during that operation, and He has blessed me for I don't have to fight the desire for drugs as many other recovered addicts do.

What did my nightmare flirtation with drugs cost me? It cost me my self-respect for awhile; activity in the Church I love; it nearly cost me my marriage and fine family; it very nearly cost me my practice and I could have been a murderer if the man I'd operated on had died because of a botched operation, and it could have cost me my life.

I'm back at the clinic operating again. I am so grateful for those doctors who forgave me, gave me a second chance and took me back.

In order to repay society for my behavior, I came forward and admitted to being a former drug addict. I now give talks to school children and organizations on the evils of drugs and of the insidious way they work. I had no idea of becoming an addict when I took the first pill, and I don't think others who tamper with drugs think they'll end up as addicts. Soon they're hooked and helpless, a slave to them. If there was ever a devilish habit in the world it is drugs! Hopefully I've helped some young people stay off drugs. I pray I have!

Saved by a Miracle

Brother LaVoy Knight passed away recently at the age of ninety. He'd been an active member of the Church all his life. During his last year, he handed out the programs at Sacrament meeting every Sunday in spite of the pain he suffered in his joints as he hobbled around to fulfill his duty. He also did his home teaching regularly and made his last visit the night before his death. He truly endured to the end.

I was born in Cleveland, Emery County, Utah in 1907, the twelfth of thirteen children. When I was seven, the family moved to Sigurd near Richfield, where Father was in the honey business. I attended grade school there and graduated from high school in Richfield. My family moved to Salt Lake City about this time, where I found employment delivering coal.

My niece, Lucille Knight, was attending BYU. Mother, who was Lucille's grandmother, invited her to our home in Salt Lake to spend Thanksgiving. Sarah Dennison, a friend and roommate of Lucille's, was invited also.

When Lucille told Sarah that her uncle was coming to Provo to take them to Salt Lake, Sarah thought the uncle would be an older man, for all of her uncles were middle-aged. She was amazed when the car pulled up and a young man, twenty, got out of the car and Lucille introduced him as her Uncle LaVoy. I drove the two girls to Salt Lake City, and during that ride, I fell in love with Sarah.

By Christmas, I had convinced Sarah that she should come to Salt Lake to work, as I wanted to be near her and the ride to Provo was a rather long one. Besides, I didn't like the idea of her being around so many handsome young men at the Y!

This was the height of the depression and I worked at whatever I could. We couldn't afford to get married then. Like many others, we couldn't pay the living expenses a family entails so we didn't marry for more than three years. We were finally married on January 9, 1932.

Sarah's father had a fine farm and I loved farming, so we moved to Salina and worked on the farm for a few years. Later, I got a good job with the railroad, bringing in more money. I worked there for thirty years, but I missed the farm and dreamed of the time when I could retire from my job with the railroad and buy a little farm.

After retirement, we moved to Vernal as our son was there. We found a fine farm, and I pursued my life-long dream of owning and working my own farm.

One nice summer day, I decided the hay was ready to cut, so I drove across the creek to where the windrower and the hay were. It was less than a mile. The windrower is a large, gas-driven machine that cuts the hay and leaves it in a neat row ready for the baler. I made one round, but the hay was heavy and it soon clogged up and stopped the machine from operating.

I took it out of gear, but left the engine running, and climbed into the machine to unclog the knife. (The knife is about twelve feet long and it goes back and forth at the speed of fifty miles a minute while a wheel with paddles about three feet apart pushes the hay into the knife.)

I unclogged the hay and was ready to get out when the vibration of the machine made it slip back into gear and the motor started again. I was caught between the knife and the wheel which was now pushing me toward the knife. *There was absolutely no means of escape. I was trapped, and I knew I faced a certain and horrible death for that knife could cut me into ribbons in seconds. Nothing but a miracle could save me. I breathed a fervent plea to my Heavenly Father as I saw the blade coming toward me with great speed. As the knife was ready to slash me, to my utter amazement and joy, a miracle happened! The machine suddenly stopped!* I sat there too stunned to move for a moment, then on shaking legs I weakly scrambled out of that death trap to discover that my arm was cut and lying open like a round of beef that had been sliced. It was bleeding profusely so I tied a red bandanna around it, shakily pulled myself into the truck and rushed to the house. My wife and I hurried to the emergency room where Dr. Durante took three hours to sew me back together. The artery had not been cut but the tendons had to be fastened. The deep cut ran from the wrist to the elbow.

Later, we went to the machine to see why it had stopped so miraculously. Strangely enough, there was my pocket knife standing up in a strategic position to lock the machine so it couldn't move. This was what had stopped the wheel from pushing me into the knife. But the question was, how did the pocket knife get into the machine to lock it?

Upon examining my trousers, I discovered that they had been cut right through the bottom of the pocket so the pocket knife could fall out in the exact place needed to stop the machine and save my life! How my trousers had been cut while my leg hadn't was a mystery until I discovered that part of the heavy, bone handle of the knife had been broken off. That was what the machine hit when my trousers had been cut and not my leg.

I know that I owe my life to the mercy of a kind Father in Heaven because that pocket knife fell into the exact place to stop the machine. Every day, I thank God for His mercy in saving me from a horrible death and for the great blessing of life and this glorious gospel.

A Great War Hero

Thomas Hawkes, Jr. endured a loveless childhood of neglect that might have crushed a person less strong and brilliant and turned him into a delinquent. Instead, he became one of our great war heroes. He also became a distinguished orthopedic surgeon and a great humanitarian.

I was born September 17, 1944, in Brigham City, Utah, to Thomas Hawkes Sr. and Ila Mae Hunt. Mother was first sergeant in the Police Department and my father was the battalion chief in the Fire Department.

I came from a family where no love or nurturing were shown. As I remember, I practically raised myself. Mother was gone most of the time and wasn't very loving when she was home. Both my parents were LDS by virtue of their families, but there was no religious teaching in our home. My only contact with the Church while growing up was through scouting. Eventually, I earned the rank of Eagle Scout.

Our home was a place of fierce and passionate quarreling and confusion. My father seemed to think that alcohol was a cure for everything. He'd given me drinks of beer and alcohol since I was three and whenever I had a cold, he'd give me a belt of liquor. I know now that both parents were alcoholics. Sometimes their fighting became so violent that guns were brandished. As a result, I stayed home as little as possible, and this was fine with my parents.

In the summers, we children were farmed out to our relatives in Richfield, working up to fourteen hours a day baling hay or thinning sugar beets. At the ripe old age of twelve, I was extremely independent. I'd been driving a pickup on the farm from the time I was about seven, so I was able to get a job as a helper at Tony Madison's fishing camp up on the Strawberry. Those who were employed there were of the rougher element. Almost all the men smoked and drank heavily.

I probably would have taken up smoking but it made me cough, and I had no desire to drink because of the disgust I felt for my alcoholic father. I was dreadfully afraid of girls, so I didn't develop many bad habits. In spite of the company there, I loved the fishing and had a rather interesting summer.

To give you an idea of how much contact I had with my family and how much freedom I had, there was practically no communication between us. They didn't ever seem to think of me or if they did, they felt I could take care of myself in spite of the fact that I was only twelve years old. I hadn't heard from them all summer.

Upon returning home for school, I went to our house, only to find that it was empty and had been sold! I felt totally abandoned. Finally, I went to the police station to find my mother. She was living on the west side of Salt Lake in a rough neighborhood. She informed me that she and my father were now divorced.

When I was sixteen, mother remarried, and there were tremendous problems in the home. Since Mom was forced to keep my two younger sisters, and I was a sophomore in high school at the time, I told her that I didn't want to create more conflict so I would leave and I'd be all right.

I didn't have a place to stay so I contacted Dad and found he was living with an alcoholic woman in a one-and-a-half-room apartment with a pull-down bed, a tiny bathroom and a small kitchenette. I realized that I couldn't stay there so all through high school, I moved around, staying in furnace rooms or any place I could. I ate the leftover food from grocery stores whose employees were kind enough to save it for me. In the summers, I took off and worked in the mountains or did farm or ranch work.

In spite of having no home, I earned a high grade point average in high school, for I had a deep desire to attend the Air Force Academy and become an Air Force officer and pilot. I worked extremely hard to achieve that goal. Much to my joy, I was given an appointment by Senator Bennett to attend the Air Force Academy after high school. In my senior year, within three months of graduation, I received a letter saying I had failed part of the entrance requirements and my appointment had been given to another young man. I was devastated! I strongly questioned the fact that I hadn't passed the exam. Although I didn't realize it then, I later found that this was a political move. My appointment had evidently been given to the son of someone who had contributed to the Senator's campaign. Later, I received a letter saying there had been a computer error and that I could apply again the next year.

I turned eighteen and had been living on the streets for two-and-a-half years. I had no assets, although I'd worked all through high school after football practice or wrestling practice. I had to have some money so I went to Wyoming looking for work. When I returned, I planned to join the military as an enlisted person although I really didn't want to. I had very few options open to me since I had no family or extended family to turn to.

I finally found work at a ranger station, working for a private contractor. My job was to spray pine trees for war beetles. I was the only one who knew how to work with animals so I was given some old army pack saddles and four mules. I filled five-gallon cans with insecticide and then took them to depot points for the crews. Later I picked up the empty cans, I picked up my provisions and camped alone. I did that all summer, and I was alone almost all of that time.

Almost every other weekend, the whole camp would go to Evanston and drink heavily and do the things men do when they get drunk. After attending one of these sessions and not participating in the activities, I found them totally disgusting so I refused to go. I preferred to stay in the mountains alone.

After I delivered the insecticide, I had some time on my hands. The skies were so beautiful. You could look up at the stars and sit and dream about other worlds and wonder about God. All through high school, I don't recall going to church or having any contact with a religion. I don't think I would have been classified as an atheist, but probably as an agnostic. I'd seen so much cruelty, deception, dishonesty, pain and sorrow in the world that I didn't believe in anything or trust anyone. *As I looked at the stars, I found myself pleading with God to let me know what direction I should take in my life.*

I knew this was just a summer job, although I was earning quite a lot of money, or so I thought. With that money, I felt I could survive and make plans for the winter. When I went to get my wages, a one-time payment at the end of the summer, the boss wouldn't pay me. I had nothing for having worked all summer. I thumbed my way back into Salt Lake. My clothing and shoes had been ruined by the insecticide. It was getting cold so I went to the Rose Park area to find a fellow I knew to see if I could sleep in his garage. He was really a wild kid, one of the gang called The Black Widows. He informed me he was going to the University of Utah on a scholarship, so I jumped on the back of his motorcycle and rode up to the University to see if I could qualify for a scholarship. I found I could easily qualify but I was too late for the fall quarter of school, so I filled out the application for the winter quarter.

I didn't know what I was going to do in the meantime. It seemed like everything in the world was stacked against me. I walked by the football field and sat there watching the team practice. I'd played two years at West, but hadn't received a scholarship. After watching the players, I felt I was better than most.

This time I think the Lord had heard my prayers, for there was a fellow named Harry James whom I'd known when we were kids. He was a star player at the University of Utah. Harry and I met when I was in high school, and he recognized me. He grabbed the coach and said, "Give this kid a try. He's the best player I ever saw in my life! He can play football as well as I can. He's a great player!" The coach took me in the back room and gave me some old equipment. They gave me some leather helmets and no base guards. I went out there with oversized pants and no pads, but after seeing me play, the coach told me I could play fullback on the freshman team. They arranged to have my tuition paid for by a booster. I was also given a scholarship for the following year. I still had the problem of no place to live so I could survive the winter.

My father had straightened up his life to some extent, and we were now friends. He told the coach that I really needed a place to live so they found me a small apartment near the University of Utah. I spent very little time in the apartment, for when I wasn't practicing football, I worked at the cafeteria at the university in the Union Building. When we weren't busy, I found that I could sit and debate on the ills of life with some of the rebellious scholars.

I took a class that was very anti-Mormon. We often debated with returned missionaries and other members of the Church. Oftentimes, we tied them up in knots, for we had a group of excellent debaters.

I was extremely wary of the hippies for they were doing a lot of drugs. Football was my salvation, so I kept a strict training schedule, not because of the Word of Wisdom, but because I knew I needed to keep my body as strong and healthy as possible in order to get through college on my football scholarship. I was made captain of the football team which was extremely satisfying. Since I had a four-point grade average I was also given a scholarship and joined Phi Beta Kappa. To my joy, I was given a job at CIE, Civic Intermountain Express, at the unheard of wage of $3.25 an hour when most people were only earning $1.00 or $1.25 an hour. People now laugh at that small wage when I tell them this, but it seemed like a fortune to me then.

I was soon earning five dollars an hour and was working about fourteen hours a day. This was the first time in my life I had money to actually buy good clothes and a can of soda pop or a candy bar when I wanted it. I didn't care for junk food much since I hadn't been able to have it, and I hadn't developed a taste for it. I had been living on discarded fruits and vegetables from Safeway and IGA, so when I had money I purchased fresh fruits and vegetables, for those were the foods I enjoyed.

I entered my sophomore year with great expectations. My father seemed to be doing better with AA, which pleased me a great deal, so I decided to splurge and I bought a motorcycle for $125 to give me transportation.

My football year was fantastic! We played Wyoming the first day and I was named defensive player of the week and was interviewed by television and was on a full scholarship the next morning. I also had a Fulbright Scholarship, which gave me some extra money. That year I received a lot of publicity. Then the University of Utah beat West Virginia. I made several outstanding plays in that game and was on television many times and in demand for interviews. I helped with the March of Dimes Telethon, and I also set up an athletic program at St. Ann's Orphanage, which gave me a big writeup in the papers. Everywhere I went people knew me and accepted me. This was such a far cry from what I'd experienced in my high school years and in my entire life before that.

I had very little use for religion, but I knew that there was definitely something missing in my life. I had all the things I'd ever dreamed of:

the champagne, the limelight, the dinners at the country club, and the use of a Corvette donated by a Chevrolet dealership. I'd worked hard for all of this, but I found that Corvettes, fancy clothes and popularity didn't really fill my needs or my hunger for something more meaningful in my life.

Christmas season was coming on, and while the world seemed to be celebrating, my father got drunk again, passed out and hurt himself badly. The Christmas carols made me sad, and I often cried myself to sleep at night, for I felt like a lost soul. When you are alone, the holidays can be the saddest time of year, for everyone else seems so happy and upbeat. That was one of the loneliest periods of my life.

I went back to school that winter quarter. Now people were watching basketball and I was no longer in the limelight. I was increasingly depressed and lonely. I felt empty in spite of the acclaim I had recently received.

I tried to obey God's commandments and I started to pray. I investigated all the Eastern religions and philosophies in an effort to find the answers for something significant in my life. I talked with my father about my feelings, but didn't get any satisfaction there.

I had my motorcycle right by my apartment. It was freezing cold but in a moment of black despair, I jumped on my motorcycle and I started driving with no destination in mind. I drove until I stopped in Mazatlan, Mexico. The road was so extremely slick that I turned my bike over. I couldn't get parts right away so I went out on the beach. I was out of money so I wired my sister to send me some money out of my bank account. She contacted the university, and they called me and arranged for me to get back to the United States and start spring quarter at the university. Most of my grades were up except for one math class where I had gone from a four-point down to a one-point average that quarter. I had to get high grades if I was going to play spring quarter. It was 1965 and the war was going on. I received a draft notice and the coaches arranged for me to join the Army Reserves. After a training cycle in Ft. Knox, Kentucky, I was to return to the university.

On the staff was a minister. We formed a close relationship and I told him that my life was a mess. He was friendly so I decided to study with him. He had a very strong testimony of Jesus Christ and I admired him while everyone else was afraid of him. Under his influence, I started reading the Bible and enjoyed it immensely, even though I was majoring in philosophy and taking philosophy classes. I'd never read the Bible before except in a religion class. It made me understand who I was and where I was going.

That winter I was writing a paper on the Mormon Church so I enrolled in a religion class on the Doctrine and Covenants. I took the scriptures to the mountains to read them and I was extremely interested. I had a Doctrine and Covenants I had taken from the Institute. It had a Book of Mormon in the front. When I returned the book to the Institute, they gave it to me and I was glad to finally have a Book of Mormon although I could not fully appreciate the words I found in those pages at that time. What impressed me was the change in the countenance of those young people as they studied and gained a testimony and then had a desire to serve their Heavenly Father in the mission field.

I knew that there must be a Creator. There was too much order in the universe for this marvelous world to just happen! I knew, from gazing at the heavens so many times, that I could not deny that there was a Creator, a Director or some divine intervention. I saw this from the laws of physics, the laws of mathematics and from the written word of such men as Shakespeare, Emerson, and Thoreau, and from the Bible.

About this time, a beautiful and exceptional girl came into my life. Her name was Ethel Christine Robinson. I had experienced so much sorrow, and now I had found joy and meaning in life. I knew that my prayers had been answered for now I was deeply in love and I would have the love and companionship of this wonderful girl. I knew I was going to Vietnam and decided that I needed to be married by the time I graduated. Ethel would only marry someone who would take her to the LDS temple. I knew that she was the girl for me so I learned Mormonism step by step by step, although I did not really understand what I was doing. I felt that when I went to the temple that all my desires for a testimony would be given to me. Needless to say, during my endowment, I was very confused and not prepared for the symbolism.

I was sealed to my wife, graduated from the University of Utah and commissioned in the United States Army, all within one week. I was immediately sent to St. Antonio, Texas, where we attended a large ward.

There were many fine, young couples in the ward who became our good friends.

For my initial training, I was sent to White School in Weatherford, Texas, where there was no branch of the Church. At the training cycle, the alarm went off at five in the morning. The rain was beating down and we were told that we would not be flying that day. I remember it was Sunday. Ethel informed me that she had found a branch fifty miles away in Wilmington, Texas, where she was going to church that morning. I gave her many excuses about the dangers of driving in the storm, but needless to say I accompanied her to Wilmington to church that morning.

Church was held in a dilapidated building in a bad part of town. As we drove up to the address, I knew this couldn't be the place. I felt sure we'd made a mistake in interrupting our sleep. *We got out in the storm, went to the door and opened it and there was a small group inside. The members were overjoyed to see us. They thought we were angels from Salt Lake City, who'd been married in the temple and had been sent from heaven! They were all converts to the Church and needed help badly. By the time church was over, I had been made the Young Men's President and was teaching a Sunday School class of two deacons and one teacher, and we had six home teaching families. I had never held a position in the Church before so this was a little alarming to me, but the Lord knew just what I needed.*

The gospel was being taught on a very basic level, about baptism, bearing one another's burdens, loving one another, repentance, and the Holy Ghost. I started to understand about the atonement of Christ and the necessity for it. They asked me many questions which I could not answer so I knew I must study.

At that time we would only fly a few hours each day, so we had many hours of waiting for our turn to fly. This allowed me to study the gospel extensively. I read the Book of Mormon thoroughly, the Doctrine and Covenants, the Bible and the Pearl of Great Price.

At the end of six months, we had a lesson on testimonies in our small branch. I urged the young men to stand and bear their testimonies. The students told me that if I would bear my testimony, they would. After they'd borne their testimonies, I didn't have the courage to stand

and bear mine. I knew they were very disappointed in me. *We had only one fast Sunday left in that branch. I was grateful that I was able to stand on my feet, and in all honesty, thank my Heavenly Father for the gospel and for His Son, Jesus Christ. I wasn't very articulate and bore my testimony in a very humble way, but I'd come a long way in a very short period of time.*

We were sent to Vietnam and landed at night. We suffered a mortar attack and a missile attack which destroyed my personal belongings and all of my side gear. In the early morning when the attack was lifted, I walked to my sunlit compound. It was unlike anything I'd ever imagined. There were palm trees and about sixteen men sitting on beach chairs, and wearing bright-colored boxer shorts or nothing at all. They had obviously been drinking all night. I approached them and they asked me if I was the new pilot. An officer asked me if I would make an emergency flight. He looked in a little better shape than the other men, but he was too drunk to fly. We ran to the helicopter. I was still in my khakis and had no gloves or helmet. I felt very uncomfortable sitting in the pilot's seat. I started the helicopter and it lifted off. He threw a map at me and gave me a set of coordinates and started talking on the radio to about five different people all at once. I couldn't understand the radio and could barely understand him. He screamed at me and said I was going to get us killed. He grabbed the stick and turned the helicopter on it's side and we fell like a rock. He was out of his mind. I wrestled him for the controls. He let out a stream of profanity which was interrupted again by a wham, wham, wham as we took rounds in the bottom of the helicopter. The emergency light went on and we could see and smell gas beginning to leak up through the floor as the tank was directly under the seats. We crash landed in a circle of personnel carriers. He was screaming at me all the time that I'd gotten us shot down. The helicopter was attracting intense fire and I could see three men lying by the personnel carriers. It was a grim scene. All of them had been hit. One of them was dead. One was a young man about my age. He was attempting to get to me when a round struck him in the back and upper chest. He fell upon me, bleeding profusely. I had to draw upon everything that I'd been taught to stop the blood. His life was leaving his body. He lay there all that day in the stifling heat and humidity with bullets and fragments flying all around. The smell of death and burned flesh was nauseating. This was my introduction to the war.

1968 was the most intense fighting in the entire Vietnam war. We were confronted constantly with battles which kept us going from one fire fight to another, picking up the injured and seeing young men die. It stimulated me to read extensively on how to treat the wounded. I never could know enough. There was always something new to be encountered. The dead were taken to a building directly across from my sleeping quarters. The smell of death was with me day and night. I was grounded for having flown too many combat hours, so my job was to wash the dead bodies and prepare them for shipment back to the United States.

I was awakened one night and asked if I was a Mormon preacher. I told the person that I belonged to the Church of Jesus Christ, sometimes called Mormons. He informed me that a young man had been seriously wounded and wanted a blessing. He said that he already had the other person to help me give it. I went to the hospital and found this young sergeant who was to help me give the blessing. He hadn't been active in the Church, but because of the terrors of war had just recently contacted the branch and wanted to become active. We rushed to the hospital. This wounded young man had a wonderful countenance. He was a returned missionary who had a wife and a baby daughter he had never seen. The jeep he was riding in had run over a mine that morning. Both his legs had been blown off at the hips. My greatest fear was to be a double amputee as this young man was. Although I didn't mind dying, I just didn't want to be maimed. He had such a testimony of Christ and of the Church. He spoke with great faith and great conviction. *We'd arranged for the sergeant to give the blessing. We anointed his head with oil, but the young man asked me to give him a blessing. I laid my hands on his head and slowly and with hesitation, started giving him a blessing. We informed him that his body would be made whole, and that this was a temporary thing. The awkwardness wore off and I felt a great warmth come over me and my hands and a feeling of comfort as if there were truly heavenly messengers there. I opened my eyes and found that the young man had died from a large blood clot that had stopped his heart.* Needless to say I was devastated, thinking that I was an unclean vessel, that I had said something wrong.

I went back to the compound and the officers said that they'd give me one last chance to have a drink with them. I went over and sat down with a glass in my hand. I thought this was something to take away the pain from my heart and my mind, only to find that when it was my turn to take the bottle, I simply couldn't. I handed back the bottle, thanked them for their friendship and walked to my bed.

I prayed to my Heavenly Father to comfort me. I received no burning bush, no angels, only the comforting thought that if I kept the commandments, I'd be all right no matter what happened to me. I read and I pondered all the next day and was soon set apart in the LDS branch as the second counselor. In humility I promised to obey all of Heavenly Father's commandments. I read and studied all I could about priesthood blessings and had many opportunities to bless young men over the next four months. The only problem I had was the gnawing loneliness from the separation from my wife.

The first of October, we had a great conference of all the servicemen in the branches. We baptized 64 young men in the South China sea with a barbed-wire fence and armed guards surrounding it. Marvelous testimonies were borne by everyone in attendance. *The spirit was so strong that you just wanted to stand up and shout Hosanna! Truly the Spirit of God like a fire was burning in each of our hearts.* It was interrupted by a call for all of the pilots to return to their bases.

The North Vietnamese army had started an offensive on the ocean border. Twenty men went in on a hillside to prepare a landing zone. As the helicopters came in, the North Vietnamese opened fire, and hit 64 helicopters in one hour. There was great artillery fire. By late afternoon, all had been evacuated except the original 120. There were fifteen survivors out of 120 men, some of whom were so seriously wounded that they could not move and were holed up in a bomb crater. We knew that we must attempt to evacuate those wounded soldiers under intense fire. In a helicopter without guns, we were sitting ducks. As I pulled up in the trees, the helicopter's warning lights were flashing. We'd been hit and the co-pilot was dead. There were no communications on the helicopter. The engine exploded and started to roll over the edge of the sheer mountain side. It took all my strength and skill to right it. I was trying to gain some speed so it wouldn't crash. I struggled to get down to the Special Forces holed up in the valley below. As we flew over an enemy bunker, they blew off the tail of the rotor of the helicopter with a rocket-propelled grenade. It started spinning, the fuselage turning equal and opposite to each revolution of the blades. As I struggled to keep it upright, I knew for a certainty that I was going to die and then all my questions about God and eternity would be answered in a matter of seconds. This knowledge gave me great comfort. The impact of the helicopter was horrendous. The jarring of the impact broke four of the vertebrae in my spine and practically all of my teeth, pushing my left ankle in a grotesque way. I sat there somewhat shocked that I was still alive and felt the rotor blade strike the earth. With the force of the impact, the jet fuel exploded, apparently within a matter of micro seconds. I felt the air being sucked from my lungs. The skin on my arms, face, neck and legs popped as I was blown through the front windshield. I sustained 40 percent burns and landed in the grass. My left eye was blinded. I couldn't see. A bullet struck my armored chest protector blowing me backward. I thought *finally I'm going to die.* I could not breathe. I thought of my beloved wife and that I hadn't had an opportunity to let her know of my love for the gospel of Jesus Christ. I was able to take off my helmet and look up at the sky. Suddenly my body was engulfed in flames. I could hear my skin popping. With extreme difficulty and horrendous pain, I rolled in the dirt to put out the flames, and crawled away from the wreckage. That is the last thing I remember until I awoke in the hospital days later.

When I opened my eyes, a pleasant-looking nurse was looking down at me. "You've finally come to," she said. "It's been 'touch and go' with you all these days, but you're going to make it."

"Am I going to be maimed?" was my first question, for I didn't fear dying, only being terribly maimed in some way.

"You were burned badly and suffered many broken bones and other problems, but we're going to fix you up. Don't worry," she said with a smile. "You were left for dead after you were brought in here. *Do you know what saved you?"*

"No," I said. "What?"

"Your LDS garments," she said. "I'm a Mormon too. You'd been left for dead but I recognized your charred garments and knew you were LDS. I felt we must give you a chance, slim as it looked, and we began

working with you instead of the other poor fellows. You can only thank God that we did."

I found that I was the only survivor among the twelve occupants of our helicopter and that I was the result of a miraculous rescue myself.

I spent the next year in the hospital before they'd give me a medical discharge, but during that year I gave the medics a bad time. I was determined to return to Asia to fulfill my commitment not more than three months after my close brush with death. It was determined that my injuries made it impossible for me to return to combat. Instead, I took the government's offer of funding my medical education and I returned to the University of Utah to attend medical school. I was a Ute again!

I graduated from the U. of U. Medical School in 1974 where I received my MD degree, and completed my internship and residency in orthopedic surgery in 1979. I completed a fellowship in children's orthopedic surgery in 1981.

In spite of the fact that doctors told him he had only half a liver and he suffered continual pain from spinal injuries he suffered when his plane went down, he accomplished more in his short years than ten ordinary men do in a lifetime. He was honored for his heroism as a Med Evac pilot and retired as a Colonel in the Army. His honors include the Distinguished Flying Cross, the Purple Heart, and the Silver Star. He served in scouting in both Europe and the U.S. and gave life-long service to The Church of Jesus Christ of Latter-day Saints where he served as a Regional Representative, on the Young Men's General Board, and in many other positions. He also gave humanitarian service in Bosnia, Croatia, China, and recently in Vietnam.

Dr. Thomas Hawkes, Jr. passed away at age 53 on Dec. 27, 1997 after courageously enduring pain from his Vietnam War-related injuries for 29 years. He leaves behind his wife, Ethel, ten children, and eleven grandchildren.

God Moves in a Mysterious Way

This is the story of a man who found the true gospel of Jesus Christ by reading a pamphlet on the subway train in New York City. He had been searching and praying for the truth for years and knew that the Lord answered his prayers the day he picked up that little pamphlet. The gospel completely changed his life and that of his family.

This is a very special day in my life for I am able to relate some of my experiences which I hope will help my brothers and sisters here on earth as I bear them my fervent testimony of the truthfulness of the gospel of Jesus Christ.

I was born in 1945 in Santurce, Puerto Rico, often called San Juan by the tourists. I was born of goodly, loving parents. When I was about two years old, my father was in a truck accident and suffered an injury to his back which made it impossible for him to do the work his job required, so it became necessary for Mother to take over the responsibility as breadwinner for the family.

I remember moving from a large house to a small, more humble home. Mother worked long hours in a glove factory. She walked about five miles to work and home again every day. My father, who had been a cook in the Navy, stayed at home and became the homemaker. My parents wanted more opportunities for their children so they decided to to come to America. They sold their little home in San Jose and took a plane to Brooklyn, New York. It was quite an experience. I still remember landing at the airport on a cold March afternoon after a twelve-hour flight on the Pan American Clipper. There was an icy breeze blowing as we walked from the plane to the main terminal. How very cold I was! That was my first memory of America.

We lived with a friend for a time until Mother was able to get an apartment. My father had stayed behind because he was in the midst of selling our small home and taking care of other business details. Mother found us an apartment in a tenement house in Brooklyn. The ghetto area in which the tenement house was located was called Red Hook. It was inhabited mainly by Dutch, German and Irish people and later by Italians, and then by Puerto Ricans. When we arrived, it was mainly inhabited by Italians. It was a difficult experience to live in this rather dangerous area. Next door was the headquarters of the Gallo family, a Mafia family. Since the Mafia was strong there, people didn't come around to steal or bother anyone on that block. I was six or seven years old at the time, and I remember that once or twice, the Gambino family, who were the enemies of the Gallo brothers, shot out the windows in all the apartments on the first floor. We happened to live on the first floor so my parents had us all lie on the floor until the shooting was over.

The apartments began to deteriorate after the Italians moved out, and it became mainly a Puerto Rican or Spanish neighborhood. The landlord did not care for the apartments properly so the rents were cheaper and a poorer class of people moved in. We were soon surrounded by burned out buildings, junkies, and bad people. As I was growing up, I remember how much I loved the movie, West Side Story, for it reminded me of my neighborhood. Instead of dancing in the mob scenes of the movie, we actually fought with bricks, bats and knives. Drunks and smut peddlers came along later.

My parents wanted a better environment for us children. I remember the burned-out buildings and abandoned junk cars on the streets. *I can say that I am thankful to my Heavenly Father, for he always kept me out of trouble. I guess I was a survivor for, as a child, I was able to go from the Latin area of the ghetto to the Italian area or the Irish area or the German side safely. I thank my Heavenly Father for my good parents. They helped me to develop a keen conscience and to know right from wrong.*

My parents wanted me to go to church although they never went to church themselves. We were Catholics, but the Catholic Church was far away. One cold and windy Christmas Eve I went to Midnight Mass at an Episcopal Church across the street from our apartment. I went in and sat alone in one of the front pews. I fell asleep. Everyone left and they closed the church with me sleeping inside. I was still sleeping when someone came back and woke me up. It was a parishioner. She said, "I thought I remembered seeing a little boy in the front pew and I was wondering where you were when everyone left. It stayed on my mind. I went home and I was home about an hour and I worried about the small boy I'd seen. I went back to the priest and he gave me the key and I came to the church to check and found you asleep." I was so glad she had remembered me, for I'd have been mighty scared if I'd awakened to find myself in that big, dark church alone.

When I returned home my parents asked me how I liked church and I said, "Oh, it's great. Even better than the Catholic Church." They asked me why and I said, "Because they speak English and I can understand what they say." I started going to the Episcopal Church, and later became a member of the executive committee of the church. Still, I never felt that I really belonged there. Naturally, when I married, my beautiful bride and I were married in that church.

I was inducted into the Army soon after I was married. I could have been sent to Vietnam as some of my buddies were, but I wound up in Ft. Hood, Texas, and after the war I returned to Brooklyn. Two years later a beautiful baby girl was born to us. Later on we had a son. My children were very important to me. We had a great family and I was devoted to them. I enjoyed being with my children, but I had marriage problems which I tried in vain to work out.

I thought about people in other religions who said that they had been "born again" and had very special, spiritual experiences. I know now that during my life, I've had some special religious experiences but I just didn't recognize them at the time. I read about people in the Bible who were able to communicate with Heavenly Father. I thought about our marriage problems. I began to realize that the best place to live the gospel is in one's own home. I thought that if I prayed to Heavenly Father about the things that were wrong in my life, I would find an answer.

I went to the bathroom of our home and I knelt down and asked for forgiveness for the things that I had done wrong in my life and had remorse for my mistakes. I asked for help in living a better life. I wanted to be better to people and I wanted to work in the church. I asked God to help me be a better father and a better husband, and for his help in bringing up my children to keep the commandments. I wanted to have family unity and love in our home. As I prayed, a special feeling came into my chest and tears started flowing from my eyes, and I could hardly believe such great joy, such great happiness that filled my heart. It was something that I had never experienced before. This great love for my family that filled my heart was unbelievable. I saw in my mind's eye that I was somewhere and all the people were dressed in white and they were beautiful people. There was a wonderful feeling of love there. A great purpose must have brought them there. They seemed to all be engrossed in reading a book. This stayed in my mind for a long time. I wondered what this vision meant. I continued to pray for an answer to this strange and wonderful thing that I had witnessed. Surprisingly, as I look back, I remember I ended the prayer "In the name of Jesus Christ, Amen."

About a week after my prayer and that spiritual experience, I got on a subway train and sat down. There were some pamphlets on the subway seat. I pushed them aside and started to read my book. *That day I couldn't concentrate on my book. My eyes started to wander until they fell again on the pamphlets. I pushed them away and went back to reading, but my eyes wandered to the pamphlets again so I picked them up and turned them over. One had a caption that said "Christ in America." I started to read it and the thought came into my mind as clearly as if my grandfather had spoken into my ear and it said, "He hasn't forgotten us." It all became clear to me. My grandfather was a Taino Indian from Puerto Rico. It made sense. There are people all over the world. Why shouldn't Christ come over here? We are the "other sheep."* I had often asked many questions in church and the priest had never had an answer for me. He told me that there were many mysteries we shouldn't delve into. Anything that they didn't have an answer for, they said was a mystery. I thought that Christ had a body of flesh and blood while on earth, but they said God, Christ and the Holy Ghost were separate but one and they were a spirit without bodies. The minister would say, "You'll find out all those mysteries when you die. Leave the mysteries alone." This didn't satisfy me. There in that pamphlet was the information that Jesus had a body of flesh and blood as we do while on the earth, and after he was crucified, he had a body of flesh and bones. I loved that pamphlet that said that God and Christ were separate beings with bodies, and the Holy Ghost was a spirit.

Then I started to read the other pamphlet. It was called The Purpose of Life. It focused on the family. It said that I could have Heavenly Father's guidance in my family life by establishing a personal relationship with Him through prayer. I have many testimonies that this is true. This has been very important in every aspect of my life and especially now where there are many important events going on in my family. At any rate, the same incredible feeling came into my chest as when I'd prayed and had that other spiritual experience. Tears started to run down my checks and I felt the same tremendous love, the same great happiness, and joy filled my heart. There I was on the subway train with people all around me, but I cried unashamedly because of the happiness I felt. I knew that this was Heavenly Father's answer to my prayers! I knew I must find this church. Finally I found the name of the Church in small letters at the bottom of the pamphlet. It said, "The Church of Jesus Christ of Latter-day Saints." I thought, "I don't know who these people are but they surely have a long name. I'm going to find out about them."

I went home that night, woke up my wife and said, "I want you to read these pamphlets." She couldn't understand why I was so excited. I said, "Let me know how you like them. Look, they are sponsoring a "Christ in America" free talk about archaeology and you know I like archaeology," so we went. As we sat in the Visitor's Center I said to myself, "I have to learn everything about this church. Someone must teach me." The following Sunday, we found the Latter-day Saint Church and met many people. It was conference Sunday. We didn't know what that was. A Spanish lady came by and she asked, "Do you want to go to Sacrament meeting?" My wife said, "Let's go," so we went. I enjoyed the young lady who spoke and the prayers. Later, a lady got up and sang and a warm feeling came over me and I said to my wife, "This is the way it should be! This is the way it should be! This is the way it should be!" After the meeting two young men came up to us. They were about six foot five inches tall. One was a bright redhead, and the other was really blond. They looked like giants to us and they were both beautiful kids. They said, "Where do you live?" I told them and they said, "Did you know that there is an LDS Church near you?" I said "No, give me the address and I'll find it."

The following Sunday we went to the Church near us. A Spanish lady came up to us and said, "May I help you?" and I said, "Yes, I want to know more about Heavenly Father. I want to learn everything about this church."

A few days later there came a knock at our door and there were two tall, blonde missionaries. We invited them in and they gave us our first lesson and taught us the gospel. I wanted to get baptized immediately, but my wife didn't want to. I told her that if she didn't want to be baptized that we'd get a divorce and I'd get baptized by myself but we should do this as a family. I said, "This is a new beginning for us as a family."

Finally my wife asked the missionaries to give her a blessing. They put their hands on her head and gave her a beautiful blessing and all of a sudden, she collapsed and fainted. The young men were alarmed. I said, "You didn't do anything wrong." Suddenly, in my mind's eye, I was out in a wasteland. It was a cloudy day and in the clouds was a yellowish amber light, and there came a personage with a horn that looked like the Angel Moroni. It seemed to mean to me that we were ready to be baptized as a family. The thought came to me that now we can be better people.

My wife said that when she collapsed she just felt as if her spirit left her body. She said she could see us from the top of the ceiling. Then she went up, up and up and there was a light and she went toward this light and there was a man dressed in a long, white robe. He said to her, "You're now ready to be baptized." She then returned to her body and recovered. She said that she felt swollen. This reminded me of the episode in the Book of Mormon about King Lamoni.

I had tears running down my checks. The missionaries were thunderstruck. Everyone cried. We were all very happy because we knew that we'd had a great spiritual experience of the divinity of the Gospel of Jesus Christ. The following week we were baptized and it was a most beautiful baptism. Everyone was happy for us. It was wonderful for me and my family to be baptized and become members of the only true and living Church on earth. I loved it.

We then prepared to go through the Temple. We were sealed in the Washington, D.C. Temple. What a thrilling blessing to be sealed together for time and eternity as a family!

Many years later, the meaning of the manifestation of the beautiful people in white I'd seen reading a book was revealed to me when I became a Temple worker in the Salt Lake Temple. While serving in the temple, I was busy in one of the rooms when suddenly that whole vision came back to me that I'd seen years before of people dressed in white and reading a book. They were very special people. I recognized that they were in the Temple and reading the Book of Mormon. It filled my heart with such indescribable joy that it was unbelievable. The spirit was so strong in the room that day that everyone there seemed to be moved to tears of joy. As these marvelous things filled my mind, a strange thing happened right at the end of the prayer. When the person who was praying said, "In the name of Jesus Christ, Amen," a glorious testimony came into my heart of the reality of Jesus Christ. For me it was a manifestation of the Spirit and a marvelous experience!

Another great blessing came to us. I had a deep yearning to go to Utah and raise our family there. One day when I walked into the Visitor's Center, we met a man who was a guide. He took us around and showed us everything. He had a beautiful wife. They were such a great missionary couple! *I found that he had been there on a mission a year or so before and he had been leaving pamphlets in subway seats, in the library, in buses and everywhere he went. He had been praying that someone would find them and that they could benefit from them, and that they would recognize that this was from Heavenly Father. The pamphlet that guided me to the Church was probably left by this great man.* This wonderful couple were from Utah and when they found out about my desire to live in Utah, they invited us to stay in their home while I became established there as a stockbroker.

We have a testimony of the gospel of Jesus Christ. How grateful we are that our son was able to fill a mission to Columbia, South America.

I flew down to pick him up and we had a wonderful time. We were able to bear our testimonies to those great people.

Our daughter had a bad first marriage and became inactive. I put her name in the temple on the prayer roll and continued to fast and pray for her, and she is now remarried to a fine young man and has become active in the Church and they are going to the Temple.

Say your prayers! They may not be answered immediately, but they will be answered. Heavenly Father loves us. He wants us to be happy!

This is the gospel of Jesus Christ. Christ is the son of God and is the head of this Church. Joseph Smith was a prophet as is Gordon B. Hinckley today, and the Book of Mormon is true. How grateful I am that I found this marvelous gospel and that my wife and children have testimonies of it also.

A Chance for Repentance

This inspirational story of Richard Ford DeJournette tells of the unhappiness that can come into a life and how, with God's help, it is possible for one to change completely if the desire to change is great enough. It also shows the happiness and peace of mind that living the commandments can bring.

My parents came from the South and settled in Brush Creek near Vernal, Utah, where Dad was a sheepman. We also had a home in Vernal. We had never had any contact with the LDS Church and knew nothing about it before coming West. Father was a good provider and Mother was an excellent homemaker. My dad had a reputation for honesty in all his dealings. He used tobacco as most everyone in the South did, and he drank occasionally, but he was a hard worker and a generous giver and lender to all.

When I was growing up, religion was not mentioned in our home. I remember my father giving donations to the LDS Church. The only thing I remember him saying about the Mormons was that if one of them did anything bad, they'd be forgiven while if he did, he'd end up in jail.

As I grew up, the patterns of my father and older brother rubbed off on me. I started smoking at an early age and did some drinking occasionally, which led me to associate with the wrong companions. This path also led me to sorrowful marriages and divorces.

When I was going to high school, I took Seminary, not because my parents told me to, but because many of the kids I knew were going. There I learned the principles of the LDS Church. I loved my teacher, Grant Vest. I'm sure he had a very good influence on me, for deep down in my heart, I wasn't without some religion. When I was alone at the sheep camp, I often read the Book of Mormon. However, I was usually around people who were of the rougher element and very irreligious.

I first met Daun Huber in 1952. The Hubers also had sheep, and our allotments joined on the forest. I fell in love with her the first time I saw her. I thought she was the sweetest and most beautiful girl I'd ever met. She also sang like an angel. She started singing as a child with her father, who played the guitar. Then she and Dorothy Luck sang duets around the entire basin. They were both so lovely and sang so well that they were immensely popular.

Something puzzled me about Daun. I always had a weird feeling that I'd known her before, and strangely enough, she told me later that she felt the same way. There was one enormous problem. She was married to my good friend. When he became ill with heart trouble and was unable to do any work, Daun worked terribly hard trying to run a sheep outfit. I helped her as much as I could.

After her husband's death, I was going to ask Daun to marry me, but her mother secretly hinted that she didn't want Daun to marry another sheep man and continue to have the hard life she'd had. I agreed with her, for the best was none too good for Daun. I knew that I'd be selfish to marry her, for her life with me would probably be difficult. I knew that she could have any man she wanted, as lovely as she was. Reluctantly, I left Vernal with a heavy heart and we went our separate ways for many years.

Needless to say, I never forgot Daun. We both married other people, but those marriages didn't work out. When our paths crossed again in Vernal, I felt it was an answer to my prayers and a dream come true for she had always been my true love. There was one big problem. I had many vices and she was religious, and I didn't feel I was good enough for her.

I knew then that I wanted a different life style than the one I'd been following. I could see that it was breaking my health and leading nowhere but down. I was alone and the evenings were long. *I started reading the Book of Mormon again and saying my prayers and asking the Lord to help me find the right path and cure me of my addictions.*

Then, for two nights in a row, I had the strong assurance that the missionaries would visit me soon, and that I would join the Church.

One afternoon, two young men knocked at my door and introduced themselves as LDS missionaries. I invited them in and told them I'd been expecting them. They stood there in stunned silence for a few minutes. They hadn't expected such a warm welcome. The two elders told me they didn't really know why they were even on my street. They had finished all of their contacts for the day and were riding their bicycles down my street on the way home. *They rode past my house and then looked at each other. Each had a strong feeling that they should go back to my home so they turned around and came and knocked at the door.*

The house reeked of cigarette smoke and there was an empty beer can on the table, but I felt their love and acceptance and I immediately admired these two young men. I shared my life story with them and *told them I felt the Lord wanted me to change my way of living. The elders said that they knew that the Lord had directed them back to my door.*

I didn't have any close friends and no relatives in Vernal at this time. Mother had moved to Orem, Utah, to live with my sister. There was only one person in Vernal that I wanted to share this very special visit with. It was Daun Huber.

She was a good member of the Church and I knew it would please her. Daun worked at the county courthouse so I called her and asked her to come to my house the following day. I told her I had someone I wanted her to meet. She came and met the missionaries and they gave me the first lesson.

As I took the missionary lessons, I threw away my cigarettes and beer. With the Lord's help I was able to overcome those bad habits ingrained since my youth. *Heavenly Father knew of my great desire to master those addictions so he gave me the strength I needed. This was a miracle to me for I'd tried to quit many times before on my own and failed. When I took God as my partner, I was able to overcome these terrible addictions.*

Another great miracle was about to unfold. Daun and I decided that we wanted to spend our lives together here and throughout eternity, and made plans to be married. I got so caught up in these plans that I even forgot the names of those two elders who had taught me. I just knew they'd brought me the greatest gifts I'd ever received, the gospel of Jesus Christ and Daun, the girl I loved!

Daun and I were married July 17, 1986. After our marriage the missionaries gave me the final lesson. Lamond Tullis, a high priest whom I'd known for years, baptized and confirmed me on October 18, 1986. I knew in my heart that I'd made the right decision. On November 30, 1986, Brother Tullis ordained the first living DeJournette Latter-day Saint to the office of a priest.

It was December 21, 1986 when Patriarch Henry Mansfield gave me my patriarchal blessing. Brother Mansfield explained to me that the words were from God, and *at times, it took him two or three days to regain his strength after giving one of those powerful blessings.*

On November 13, 1987, Daun and I were sealed in the Provo Temple. Brother Frank Walker, who had been Daun's Seminary teacher in high school, sealed us. Elder Arden Hacking, a good friend, stood proxy for Rex Huber, Daun's deceased son, and he was sealed to us forever. What a glorious experience our temple marriage was!

In 1987 I had neck surgery. Glen Hatch, my brother-in-law, and the elders gave me a blessing before surgery. The surgery went without incident. On December 10, 1987, Daun had a modified radical mastectomy. By our faith and God's blessings, she has recovered from cancer.

I realize how precious my testimony is. Through humility, faith and prayer, it has grown. I know a testimony is something we receive as a gift, and that each individual receives his own. How wonderful it would be if I could give some of my friends the same strong testimony I have, but it cannot be given to another unless they are willing to accept it.

When my wife, Daun, and I took on a seven-year project of writing our book, *One Hundred Years of Brown's Park and Diamond Mountain,* my testimony grew even more. *Many nights I've watched Daun kneel several times in one evening, often with tear-stained cheeks. She would pray and then return to the computer and be able to find the help she needed. She had faith the Lord would soothe her frustrations and help her with the writing of the stories and her prayers were answered. I watched as she received answers to her prayers many times. I also spent a great deal of time on my knees in prayer asking our Heavenly Father to help us in our endeavor. We're so grateful that our prayers were answered, for without our Savior's love, we could never have accomplished this.*

I want to give my testimony of my feelings for the Church. What a great and glorious blessing it is to have something to look forward to in the hereafter. *It is wonderful to know that here on earth when we feel uncertain and face problems, we can get down on our knees and ask God for guidance, and he will help us for he hears and answers prayers. I know that with all my heart! He has surely answered mine and enriched my life immeasurably.*

When I go to Sacrament meeting and see those clean young men in their white shirts and ties as they pass the Sacrament, I realize what I missed as a lad. I wish that all young men could have the blessing and privilege of being taught the gospel in their youth. Sacrament meeting is also special because the speakers inspire me to strive each day to be more like Heavenly Father.

I'm not fluent in quoting the scriptures, but I'm convinced that if we strive to follow the teachings of the Gospel of Jesus Christ, we can one day dwell in God's kingdom. Christ is the head of this Church and we have the privilege of helping Him build it up, and in so doing, our testimony is built also.

Thank you, God, for allowing me to find the way and giving me a chance for repentance at the age of sixty-five. How grateful I am for my wonderful wife and for being accepted into the only true Church on the face of the earth.

A Blessing from Rush-hour Traffic

This thrilling conversion story shows how God sometimes gives us great challenges in order to get our attention. Using the rush-hour traffic, he caused Dick Stoeltzing to visit the Oakland Visitor's Center to wait out the traffic jam. This led to both his conversion and that of his wife, Judy. Dick finally found the answers to questions about life and death that he'd had all his life! Judy tells the thrilling story of their conversion.

I went to the Oakland Temple recently, and after attending two sessions, I waited in the Visitor's Center for my husband, Dick, to pick me up. He'd had meetings all day near the San Francisco airport. A lovely older sister missionary and I struck up a conversation. Our discussion finally got around to the heavy traffic in the Bay Area. She was from a small Idaho town and couldn't get used to the congestion. It was then that I told her our conversion story and why we had that "darn Bay Area traffic" to thank for our being members of The Church of Jesus Christ of Latter-day Saints.

As I look back on our nearly 28 years as members, I am grateful for the Lord's hand in our lives. Even as far back as choosing where I would attend college, He was there. I grew up in Silver Springs, Maryland, and had planned on attending West Hampton College, part of the University of Richmond in Virginia. At the time that I was accepted, I would have had to live off campus. When a high school teacher told our class about his alma mater, I took a brochure, applied and was accepted at Davis and Elkins College in Elkins, West Virginia. *During my first visit to the campus, in the spring of 1959, I remember standing by the girls' dorm and having a strong feeling as if words were coming into my mind, that I should not worry about going to any other school. It was during my freshman year that I met my husband-to-be. I never expected to go to West Virginia to marry a boy from Brooklyn, New York, but that's the way the Lord works sometimes.*

Dick and I were married in December of 1962 in the same room of the Jamaica, New York, Presbyterian Church in which his parents were married. I had been raised a Methodist, but rebaptism was not necessary to become a Presbyterian. Dick had been a senior in college when I was a freshman, and when we married, he was a Lieutenant in the Navy, serving aboard the first nuclear-powered aircraft carrier, the USS Enterprise CVA(N)-65. I followed Dick and the ship around the Mediterranean Sea the summer of 1963 as they went from Lisbon to Lebanon. Dick's obligation to the Navy was complete when we returned to Norfolk, Virginia, but he accepted a "shore duty" assignment at Moffett Field, California, so we could see America. We drove west that December.

Though the assignment was only for two years, we bought a home when we found out that I was pregnant. Our son, Jim, was born in October of 1964. While at Moffett Field, Dick met a Navy buddy who was selling life insurance. Jerry Halverson claimed that Dick would be a natural, and he was right. Dick successfully sold insurance on the side until he left active duty. He then began selling life insurance full time. We were very blessed. We occasionally attended the local Presbyterian church. Dick's new career looked promising and our second child was due in August of 1966.

In May of 1966, Dick had discomfort and swelling that drove him to the doctor's office. It turned out to be a testicular tumor, and two operations later, the doctors could not promise that Dick would live five years. We were broke and facing the expense of having a baby with no insurance. We were just out of the Navy and Dick's new job had a twelve-month maternity clause.

Dick weighed 123 pounds by the time his second surgery was over. I was nearing my ninth month of pregnancy, and I outweighed him by nearly twenty pounds! We survived the financial challenge, and our second healthy, beautiful son, Casey, joined the family. We felt a deep debt of gratitude to our Heavenly Father.

I expressed my gratitude by becoming very active in the Presbyterian Church's programs. Dick became an elder in the church, but he also began looking into other religions. Our pastor had visited Dick in the hospital, and when Dick asked him what death would be like, the pastor frankly told Dick that he did not know. The doctors had prepared Dick for the real possibility that he would die young, and Dick felt that there had to be a better answer. He began talking to Jewish rabbis, Jehovah's Witnesses, and anyone else who wished to tell him about their beliefs.

Dick was in such a frame of mind when he found himself in Oakland's rush-hour traffic. Through frustration or, looking back, we believe it was inspiration, he lifted his eyes from the snarled traffic to a beautiful building on a hill above downtown Oakland. He headed for it to wait out rush hour. A missionary couple at the Oakland Temple Visitor's Center was just finishing the last tour of the day by showing the movie, "Man's Search for Happiness." Dick was invited to watch. In his words, "It was everything I had always believed but had never been taught." He asked to see it again and was amazed that they sweetly complied. "No one ever does anything for anyone after five o'clock in a large city," this New York boy had always assumed. They invited Dick to sign the guest register and he did.

When the first set of elders called him, Dick asked me to join their discussion. I refused, feeling very fulfilled as a Presbyterian. He met with them at his office. Although Dick felt comfortable with all they taught, he did not choose to join. A second set called about a year later with the same results.

During this time Dick had remained in the Navy Reserves, and on one of his monthly "Weekend Warrior" assignments, he began talking to Tom Medford, Petty Officer First Class in his Moffett Field Squadron. Tom was in the LDS Mission presidency of his stake in Oakland. Dick was very impressed with the way Tom conducted his life, and, at Tom's encouragement, Dick agreed to talk to yet another set of missionaries. Dick asked me to be polite and listen with him.

Four months before these elders called on us, I had decided to stop smoking as a Father's Day gift to my husband. He had long wanted me to quit, but when he told me that I couldn't hope to be a healthy grandma if I continued smoking, it only took one look at my parents to know he was right. Although I had gone four whole months without cigarettes, I was afraid that I would reach for them to relieve my stress if Dick were to be sick again.

No one had prepared me for the impact of the elders' message. They challenged me to read parts of the Book of Mormon and pray to "my" Heavenly Father for confirmation about what they had taught. That evening, I knelt by our bed and said my first out-loud, from-the-heart prayer. I got up from that prayer with a sure knowledge that this was the Gospel of Jesus Christ, and I told my husband that I planned to be baptized and would he like to join me!

Our Christmas present that year was our December 13 baptism. The next day our boys were blessed, and we officially became members of Santa Clara First Ward. We were sealed as an eternal family in March of 1971. Oh, how I would love to find Elder Brent Gooch and Elder Thomas Morello and express my gratitude to them for serving missions and for teaching us the gospel.

The impact on our family joining the true church has been tremendous! Both Jim and Casey became Eagle Scouts, served honorable missions, and have been married in the Temple. I believe that my life began the day I was baptized. As I get older, I cling to this logic: instead of being 56, I'm only 28!

As I finished my story to my new-found friend in the visitor's center that day, Dick came into the Visitor's Center grumbling about the terrible mess the traffic had been. I kissed his check and bid the sweet sister missionary good-bye saying, "I'll remind him of 'The Blessing of Rush-hour Traffic.' In fact, today's traffic is probably full of families just like us."

As a Seminary teacher, it is my privilege to bear my testimony every day of the truthfulness of the incredible gospel of Jesus Christ and to thank Him publicly for patiently offering and re-offering me the great gift of membership!

Divine Intervention

The Schirners, Fred and Blue Bell, had always been looking for the true church as the Church of England to which Blue belonged didn't give them the answers they were looking for nor did other churches they investigated. One day some friends invited them to hear the Mormon missionaries. They found the true Church and the answers to the questions that had bothered them for so long.

When we were married, Fred had no religious ties in particular, although his mother had told him that the true church was out West somewhere, and when he found it he should join it. Apparently she had been exposed to the LDS Church in Germany before she came to this country.

I grew up as a member of the Church of England, and attended a Church of England boarding school. I was searching even then, and during religion classes, I asked many questions and the answer I always received was, "You must take it on faith," with no explanation. I continued to keep on searching for the answers for I felt dissatisfied and unfulfilled.

Fred and I met and were married in 1960 in the Christian church that I was attending at the time. This church didn't provide the answers so we continued to visit a variety of churches, and finally joined the Unitarian Universalist Church. The minister turned out to be very dishonest, so again, we continued to search.

Some of the questions that bothered us were: The three-in-one theory of the Christian churches; that the Father, Son, and the Holy Ghost are separate but one, and that they are spirits. We couldn't understand why Christ had come to earth and received a body, died and was resurrected and then became a Spirit. What happened to his body?

We couldn't believe that one is saved by faith alone when it says many times in the Bible that faith without works is dead. Frankly, we found the teachings of orthodox Christian ministers very confusing—a mystery that even they didn't understand.

We also didn't believe that a baby or small child would go to hell because it hadn't been baptized because Christ said, "Suffer the little children to come unto me, for of such is the Kingdom of Heaven." These and many things taught by Christian churches bothered us. We simply couldn't accept them.

The Jehovah's Witnesses had pestered us for a long time so when we saw some Mormon missionaries, we thought they were Jehovah's Witnesses and refused to talk with them.

In 1969 we moved to Minnesota and found that all school children had to attend religion classes once a week, either Catholic or Lutheran or none. We chose none, and decided to teach our three children from the Bible until the true church could be found.

Within a month of our decision, we were invited to meet the LDS missionaries by some friends whose children were being taught by them prior to baptism. The first meeting was more or less a scripture chase, and Fred was not impressed, but I invited the missionaries to dinner the following week as they impressed me. When they arrived, one of them had been transferred and in his place was the largest fellow we'd ever seen. He was about 6'10" and a former high school football player and wrestler. He made a huge impression on our two boys!

We asked all of the questions which had bothered us for years and all were answered to our satisfaction. How happy we were to find a Church which believed that God and Christ had bodies and that the Holy Ghost was a spirit; that they were separate personages; that infant baptism was wrong; and that one couldn't be saved by grace alone, but by faith and works, for faith without works is dead. We had no problem with the Joseph Smith story of his vision and the fact that he was the Lord's chosen prophet to bring forth the true gospel. We knew that there were prophets in ancient times so it only seemed reasonable that there should be a living prophet on the earth at this time.

We gladly accepted the gospel that the elders taught. It seemed so logical. *Elder Campbell asked if he could bear his testimony to the truthfulness of the gospel. He bore the most sincere and spiritual testimony I've ever heard, and it really touched our hearts. We both had such a burning in our bosoms that we felt we were on fire and when he concluded, we were totally exhausted. We'd received the answer to our prayers for we knew without a doubt that we'd found the true church at last!*

At the next meeting with the missionaries, we asked them when we could join the Church. They were shocked, for they'd had a difficult time making converts in Minnesota. They arranged to meet us at the LDS Church the next Sunday, which was a fifty-mile trip. They wanted us to learn more about the Church before baptism. It was Fast Sunday. We arrived to be greeted by a very friendly Panamanian and his wife. He and our youngest son had a lot in common, including the name Ed.

The children went to Sunday School and Primary and I attended Relief Society while Fred attended Priesthood. Then we both went to adult Sunday School and of course, Sacrament meeting where we heard many sincere testimonies. As we were leaving the Church, our son Ed asked if we would be coming back next week. Fred said that we'd be back for we'd found the true Church after a long search. I agreed with him.

The missionaries returned and gave us the remaining lessons and also continued to teach our children on their level so that they could understand the gospel and make a choice about joining the Church. We were baptized on the 16th of February, 1972, in Cass Lake, Minnesota, an Indian Branch. Ed, our youngest, was really put out because he was too young to be baptized. He said he knew the Church was true but he was only seven. Elder Campbell gave him his name and a blessing the next Fast Sunday and that seemed to satisfy him.

Fred and I and our family have been active in the Church ever since our baptisms. How grateful we are for the gospel of Jesus Christ in our lives and in the lives of our children, and how truly thankful we are that we found the true church while our children were young enough to be raised in it and taught its precepts.

When we accepted a mission call to the Philippine Islands, we saw a different side of life than we'd ever experienced before. There was such extreme wealth and extreme poverty and so many virulent diseases. We mainly worked with the poor and humble.

My husband was asked to give blessings to a group of members who all had very active cases of tuberculosis. Most of them were coughing up blood and they wiped their hands on their handkerchiefs before shaking our hands. *The Lord blessed us for we never caught the disease.*

Another time we went with the District President to give a blessing to a very sick man. He had been ill only for a couple of days, but had been told by the doctor that he was suffering from spinal meningitis and had a fever of more than 105 so he was in a very contagious stage. The District President gave him a blessing and told him that he would recover if he would take his medicine and follow the doctor's orders, although he was so terribly ill that his recovery seemed impossible at the time. *He did survive and we were spared that terrible disease, for which we thanked our Father in Heaven.*

We always talked with the children and carried suckers for them. We held the hands of a beautiful little girl. Then we noticed that her eyelids and nose had a strange-looking white skin on them. Her neighbors told us that she had leprosy. Through our District President, she was able to get treatment at the local clinic and the dread disease had begun to recede by the time we were transferred. *Again, the Lord took care of us and we didn't get leprosy. I know that He had other work for us to do, and He watches out for His missionaries. We are so grateful for His love and care.*

We traveled on concrete roads in our small Toyota Corolla. It seemed that the Filipinos were always digging up the roads and redoing them because of the deterioration caused by the salt air. They broke the concrete into large pieces which they stored on the road in huge piles with no warning signs to let one know they were there. On the winding road where you didn't know what was around the corner, this was very dangerous.

One day we'd gone up to San Miguel to teach some inactive members, and we returned about 10 p.m. on a very dark night. We remembered that they were doing the usual road demolishing when we'd passed them that afternoon. We followed a truck as it was easier to drive the fifty-some miles back to our apartment with their bright lights to guide us. We evidently picked the wrong truck to follow that night for it turned off, leaving us on the winding road with our less than adequate headlights. We rounded a corner and immediately ahead of us was a huge pile of concrete. It hadn't been there earlier in the afternoon. I braked frantically and screamed, "We're going to hit it." A collision seemed inevitable for we were going at a rather high rate of speed. Strangely enough, it didn't happen. *The car was stopped by an unseen hand and pushed backward and we were safe. We sat there for a few minutes in stunned silence. Then we gave grateful thanks to God for our deliverance for we would have surely hit the concrete without His divine intervention.* As we continued our journey to our apartment, another truck passed us and we followed it right to the locked gates in front of our apartment.

On the way to the USA after our mission was finished, we had to change planes in Tokyo, Japan. As we were leaving the plane, we heard the pilot tell one of the stewardesses that we were lucky to have made it as far as Japan because there was something seriously wrong with the plane. I know why we made it. There were eight returning missionaries on board the plane and He wanted us to all get home safely for He had work for us to do here on earth!

We know that the LDS Church is true and that Joseph Smith was a true prophet and that we have a prophet on the earth today, President Gordon B. Hinckley. We know Jesus is the Christ, the son of God, and he heads this Church.

The Power of the Priesthood Made Manifest

Brother Charles Beede and his lovely wife, Carol, are stalwarts in our ward and in the Church. Brother Beede has been a Seminary teacher for 34 years, and has been a great influence for good on the lives of hundreds of young people. Sister Beede has worked in all of the auxiliaries of the Church. Brother Beede is now Bishop of the Uintah Care Center Branch and bringing happiness to many people there while Sister Beede graciously assists.

Sister Beede tells of a very traumatic event in her life and the spiritual experience she had.

Fourteen years ago, we were anxiously anticipating the arrival of our fifth child; however, it was only my second pregnancy. Our first three children were adopted.

Things had not gone well from the beginning. I had a problem with *placenta previa,* and further into the pregnancy I was troubled with premature labor. The doctors ordered complete bed rest for the majority of the pregnancy.

After several frightening episodes of hemorrhaging, this little spirit decided he could no longer postpone his arrival. Just after midnight, June 22, exactly three months before his scheduled birth date, I was rushed to the hospital. Upon arrival, I was taken directly to the delivery room. My mental and physical state at that time was one of panic and fear. My body trembled from head to foot, and my heartbeat was faster than the baby's.

The doctors told us that the baby would stand a better chance of survival if we could buy enough time before delivery to Life Flight me to the University Medical Center Neonatal Facility. *At this point, I decided it was time for the Priesthood to take over. I asked my husband and the Bishop to give me a blessing. The administration was short but powerful. I received a calm assurance from Heavenly Father that all would be well. What a marvelous experience it was to feel the fear and panic rush from my body and be replaced with that sweet, calm peace from a loving Heavenly Father!*

When the Life Flight medical team arrived and were preparing me for the flight to Salt Lake City, they were amazed at my calmness. They told me that most patients in my condition were absolutely panic-stricken. *Of course, the difference was that I knew that Heavenly Father was watching over me as well as the sweet little spirit who was about to make his debut. I knew all would be well.*

Our son was delivered by Caesarean section June 22, 1985, at 4 p.m. He weighed a whopping two pounds, which was more than the doctors had expected. After two months in the Neonatal Unit, we were able to bring him home a month earlier than anticipated. He weighed 4 lbs 6 oz. the day we brought him home. He is now approaching his fourteenth birthday. What a wonderful blessing he has been in our lives, and how grateful I am to the Lord for looking down and taking care of both of us!

The Lord Guided Me to Our Son

Christmas gifts may come in strange ways, but the greatest gift Steven Eaton's family will ever receive came about because of an accident which nearly cost the life of their son, Nicholas. In spite of this, his family say in unison that the Christmas of 1999 was the best they ever experienced, for they still have Nicholas with them. They were far from home that Christmas, eating in a hospital cafeteria and sleeping in strange beds. In spite of that, his family will be eternally grateful that the life of their precious son was saved.

On October 14, 1999, Nicholas, who was nearly eight years old, received his mother's permission to go across the street from their Rexburg, Idaho, home to the school playground to play until dinnertime.

When he didn't return at dinnertime, his mother, Ivonne, began to worry, for he was an obedient child and such behavior was unlike him. After a search of the neighborhood yielded nothing, she became alarmed and called her husband, Steve, at work. He and his co-worker, Craig Hanni, drove around for an hour or so, looking for the boy at friends' homes and favorite haunts. When they couldn't locate Nicholas, their concerns turned to real fear.

By this time it was dark, and a cold wind had come up which had dropped the temperature to below freezing. The police were notified and the men found a flashlight. Then Hanni went to his home to get his cell phone so they could keep in touch with Nicholas's mother and wouldn't have to keep driving home to see if the boy had wandered in. "I didn't fear that Nicholas had been kidnapped, but I knew that something dreadful was wrong. I tried to keep the fear I'd felt since the start of the search from turning to panic, but I knew that it was critical that we find our son soon."

While Hanni was gone for the phone, Steve prayed fervently for help. He knew that they couldn't find his son without help of a higher kind. Immediately he received an urge to go to the construction site on the far end of the school. A new housing project was under construction and contractors were laying water mains and sewer lines in preparation for the subdivision to be built there. The Eatons found out later that many of the neighborhood children played on the construction site, viewing it as part of the school playground.

Now the question was where to look on the more than 200 acres of churned-up land. Steve Eaton said that the higher power did take over as they entered the site. "It was almost like hearing a voice in my head saying, Turn left, turn left again. Go here." Steve stepped out of his car, turning off the engine so he could hear, and leaving on the lights so he could see. At the bottom of a trench, he saw a slab of clay about the size of a queen-sized mattress. "Hey, Craig, look at this," he hollered. Then a querulous little voice said, "Daddy." To the father's amazement, he saw his son's small hand sticking out from under the slab, the only part of him that was not pinned down by the heavy chunk of clay.

All efforts to move the large slab by Steve Eaton failed. Most of the weight rested on the child's right leg and buttocks. The slab created a pocket around his head and he wasn't completely crushed into the ground.

While Craig Hanni went for help, Steve Eaton curled up with Nicholas so his legs and shoulders were under the slab, able to touch his child who was terrified that the slab was slipping and would crush him deeper and deeper into the ground.

"I promised him that I wouldn't let it slide down on him," Steve said. "I don't know whether it was from fear, or if the slab was really moving that frightened him so." The boy put his head on his father's arm, but he was slipping into shock. Steve kept touching him to assess the damage. "Can you feel that? How about that?" Nothing.

Rescuers assembled quickly, although to Steve it seemed like hours. The police, the fire department, the search and rescue unit and the ambulance arrived in force.

The question was how to remove the clay without further damaging the child. They decided that they couldn't lift it without the risk of large chunks breaking off, slipping and falling on the boy. They decided to shave away on it with a small jack hammer. It would still be a risky job. The entire crew was gathered around in case they had to grab the slab in a hurry.

His father got just as close to his son as he could. It took almost half an hour to get the boy out. The child was rushed to Madison Memorial Hospital where X-rays showed the boy had "compartment syndrome," where pressure builds up in a crushed limb. Once the pressure is removed, intracellular fluids like potassium are released into the blood at levels that can become toxic. The doctors slit the boy's skin, making four long gashes on his legs to allow the muscles to bulge and blood flow to resume. His kidneys had overloaded in an attempt to clear his blood of the poisons his dying muscles produced. His potassium level more than doubled to 9.5. People usually die when the level passes 7.

They stabilized the boy as best they could, then put the family on a medical airplane and rushed them to Primary Children's Medical Center in Salt Lake City, Utah. His parents were warned that he might die during the flight.

Friends and family gave great support, although they could do little but pray. Some drove to Utah to be a support through surgeries and waiting periods. School friends and teachers visited. *The boy received a blessing from members of his LDS faith.*

"Miraculous things did happen," according to his father. Doctors had planned to pull a vein to replace the crushed femoral artery in Nicholas's groin. Instead, they were able to fix it. Still, his condition was critical. His kidneys were having a difficult time keeping pace with his body demands so he went on dialysis.

Through those roller-coaster days, Steve Eaton, the faithful father, slept just inches from his son, returning to Idaho briefly to take care of family matters that couldn't wait. His parents came from California to be with the boy, and Ivonne Eaton's mother watched Nicholas's baby brother, a toddler.

For weeks, doctors had to sedate Nicholas to change his dressings twice a day—a painful process which still left the medicated boy screaming in agony.

According to Steve, his progress has been marvelous and mystifies the doctors. "Our son is standing, his skin grafts are doing beautifully, and his prognosis is great. I don't feel that I could ask for much more than what we've gotten from the Lord. Most people would have died, and he's still alive and getting well. Nicholas is a fighter. He wants to go home and he's getting better.

"Maybe he's alive to show others that miracles still happen. A lot of people have been praying and fasting for him. There are few ways to get the Lord's attention better than to have masses of people praying for a single cause."

An Out-of-body Experience

When Cory George had this traumatic near-death experience, he discovered the Lord had work for him to do here so he returned to this world from his out-of-body experience. He said of this, "One thing this taught me and my whole family is to no longer fear death. My short time in the 'after-life' was one of the most pleasant times I've ever experienced."

It was Friday night and I was happy that a most difficult and stressful week was over. As I drove home from work that night in the gathering darkness, I hummed a little tune. I was anxious to get back to my warm home, my loved ones, and the delicious food that I knew awaited me. It was raining and a cold wind had come up.

Suddenly an enormous truck came thundering down the hill. To my horror, it was on the wrong side of the road and was coming straight toward me. The brakes must have gone out and the driver had lost control of the huge vehicle. I swerved the car to the right in an effort to avoid a head-on collision with the truck. I knew that a deep ravine lay in that direction, and that I'd rather take my chances there than with that monster truck hitting me. But it was too late—I felt a horrible impact, and then nothing else until I awakened.

I felt so strange—as if something was being drawn from my body, and I was shooting down a long, dark tunnel of some kind. Suddenly I came out of the tunnel into a bright yet mellow light and a warmth that was difficult to describe. I felt completely encircled by warmth and peace. It was something foreign to anything I'd ever felt or known. *Where am I,* I wondered.

A kindly-looking man welcomed me. "I'm your mother's brother, William. I've come to take you to see the family. We've all been waiting for you, for we knew you'd be here today. A group of relatives and friends have gathered to meet you." I still don't know whether he actually spoke to me or whether we communicated with our minds. Things were so different there, but we understood each other's thoughts perfectly.

I looked around at the breathtaking scene before me. Everything was so bright and beautiful! The flowers and foliage were the most spectacular one can imagine. They seemed three-dimensional, and there was a warmth and a quiet peace that permeated everything, including my body and my heart!

I must have seemed puzzled as I looked at this stranger, for the man said, "You don't know me. I passed through the veil when you were just a baby. Follow me." So that was what had happened to me! I'd passed through the veil as he had. Was I dead? I surely didn't feel dead.

I followed the tall, handsome, young fellow. We seemed to float for I don't believe my feet touched the ground, but we soon came to a group of pleasant-looking people. When they saw me, they came toward me with happy, smiling faces. To my great delight, I recognized some of them. One was my mother. She was the first to reach me. "Oh, Mark," she cried. "I'm so happy to see you. How have you been, and how is Marcy and the children?" Then my father came toward me, smiling. What a reunion we had. I met my grandparents and all my departed relatives, and we had a happy time getting to know each other. Some, who said they'd come to America from foreign lands, I understood perfectly. Supreme joy and a peace beyond description seemed to fill my soul.

Soon my uncle, the young man who'd brought me there, joined the group. "You aren't to stay this time," he said pleasantly.

"Must I go back?" I cried. "It is so wonderful here."

"Tell your friends and relatives goodbye and I'll show you something that will let you know that you must return."

I reluctantly told those loved ones goodbye and then turned to William. "Look," he said, and the scene changed. "Can't you see how much your wife and children need you? You'll return to us when your work on earth is finished." I saw my wife and young children mourning in the hospital waiting room. They were crying and praying for my recovery. I knew that I must leave this wonderful place and return to my family.

I was told later what happened in the operating room of the hospital. The doctors had just finished the operation on my brain in an effort to try and relieve the pressure caused by the tremendous blow I'd received during the accident. Then I seemed to go into cardiac arrest. The doctors worked frantically for some time to save my life. Finally I heard one say, "I believe he's gone. No pulse, no respiration rate, no blood pressure, nothing! There's one thing we haven't tried. I'm going to give him a shot of adrenaline directly into the heart muscle to try to jump-start his heart."

"What good would that do? He's going to be brain damaged if he lives with that extensive trauma he's had to his brain. You said we didn't remove all the pressure," another doctor argued.

The brain surgeon ignored the advice of his colleagues and accepted the hypodermic needle filled with adrenaline and plunged it directly into my heart. To the doctor's great amazement, my heart started beating, irregularly and erratically at first, then it settled into a more rhythmic beat.

Suddenly I awoke on the operating table to the most excruciatingly painful experience of my life. The mammoth pain in my head felt as if it was literally killing me. Never have I felt such piercing pain! I must have screamed, for the doctor immediately gave me a shot of some strong pain killer that put me out. I awoke later with the same horrible, throbbing pain that continued, to some extent, for days in spite of valiant attempts of doctors and nurses to alleviate it. How grateful I was when the pain somewhat subsided.

My wife told me later that the elders had come along while I was in the emergency room, just before the surgeons arrived. They gave me a blessing in which I was promised I would live and be able to finish my work on earth. I'm sure if the doctors had heard that blessing, they would have scoffed, such was my condition when I was brought in, but their prediction came true. How thankful I am for that blessing and the Priesthood!

"You're a fortunate man," my doctor told me later. "We thought you were gone once, for we could find no vital signs. How that shot of adrenaline to the heart brought you around is quite remarkable when all vital signs had ceased! Our team was ready to stop trying to bring you around, but somehow, I decided to take that drastic measure as a last resort, and I'm thankful I did!"

As I think back on that out-of-body experience with great pleasure and amazement, I know that it has changed my life. I realize that my work here isn't finished and I must make the most of the time allotted me here. I want to be found worthy to be with my wife and children and those great people who have passed beyond to that marvelous place. It has also made me appreciate my life here a great deal more. Everyday with my wonderful wife and children is a bonus and a blessing that I could have missed.

Another great blessing is that it has also taken away all fear of dying. That blessed family reunion I had with my loved ones was so comforting to me that I look forward with great expectation to experiencing it again. I know how happy my loved ones are there and I'm looking forward to the day when I'll join them for another great family reunion, and we will be together as a family forever!

The Lord Protects His Missionaries

Larry and LuAnne Searle are faithful members of our ward. They've raised a fine family and were privileged to go on a mission. While there, they had this frightening experience and narrow escape which they attribute to a miracle. LuAnne tells of their harrowing and yet thrilling experience.

With our family of six children grown and doing well, much to our delight Larry and I were called on a mission to the small town of Smithers, in British Columbia, Canada, in the summer of 1996. This had been a lifelong dream to fill a mission together after our family was raised.

While Vernal is known as an inland city, and Utah is rather dry country, Canada is a much different country. It is known as the land of a million lakes and is great lumber country. It rains often, and because of this a thick and tall growth is everywhere, even alongside the road. This is called the bush.

One day we'd traveled east from Smithers to Houston, B.C. to visit the Swenson family and present a home Primary lesson to the three Swenson children and their neighbors. I might explain that Brother Swenson was from a good LDS family. In fact, his father was very active, but the son had a problem with the Word of Wisdom. As a result, they didn't send their children to Church.

The Primary president in the south area held a big activity in the summer. The Swensons' children had come, and had brought some neighbor children the year before, so in hopes of getting both the parents and the children active, we were anxious to teach their children. We had arranged with the parents that we would come to teach their children, and any other children that wanted to attend were welcome.

After giving the lesson to the children, we had a pleasant visit with the parents and were told the salmon were coming up the river past the Swenson home to their spawning ground. We thought this would be very interesting and a sight worth seeing so we decided to turn south toward a bridge to see it. We were talking and missed the turn-off. As we saw another little road further down, we drove down this road, hoping to see the river and the salmon.

We both had on our seat belts, but I was leaning forward as we were going up an incline, and I was trying to see what lay ahead. The thick bush was so overgrown it was almost impossible to see what lay to the side of us. All one could see was the road ahead. Suddenly I saw a house at the end of the road. I started to say that this wasn't the right way, when, without any warning, through the dense underbrush rushed a freight train! It was just a few feet in front of us, and it looked as if we were going to be hit by the huge train before we could possibly stop! There had been no whistle or warning of any kind because this wasn't a regular crossing.

Our car stopped with a jolt! I felt angry with my husband because it frightened me so much and I turned to say he shouldn't have teased me that way, but from the look of disbelief on his face, I could tell that he was just as stunned and surprised as I was. He was slumped in the corner with his eyes wide with astonishment.

I knew it hadn't been a joke and asked how he could have stopped so fast. He said, "I didn't." We looked at his foot and it was on the brake and clear to the floor board. He had no recollection of even touching the brake. *He knows that someone else pushed his foot down on that brake just in time to keep us from being killed. We felt that Someone in a higher place had put on the brakes, for Larry was still in shock.* He hadn't had time to even think of stopping when that great train rushed in front of us out of nowhere.

We knew that we had been part of a miracle! We sat there for a while in silence and reverence, humbly thanking God for our miraculous escape from death.

As we traveled back home, we talked about the frightening incident and the near-accident that we'd had. We don't have trains in our city and had forgotten to be aware of the tracks that lay along the highway. There was no crossing sign because it was private property.

We knew the Lord had spared us to continue our work on this earth. He had more for us to do here, and we were humbled and so grateful that He or His angelic servants had saved us from a horrible death. There would be no terrible message sent to our family waiting at home.

I know with a greater testimony that the many prayers that are offered in behalf of missionaries are answered in ways that touch their lives for good.

Visions Bring Comfort

This is a story I heard as a child and it was so dramatic that I've never forgotten it. It tells of the dream that helped convert Victor S. Showalter and of the great spiritual experience he had after the traumatic death of his wife and three of his children.

Victor Stonewall Showalter was born in 1870 in Iowa into a large family. His parents were southerners who had a plantation in Virginia and many slaves. During the Civil War, it was destroyed by the fighting that went on in that area. Disillusioned by conditions after the war, the family migrated to Iowa where they had land holdings.

There was a great call to "go West" for young men in those days for that was where opportunity seemed to lie. Victor's oldest brother, DeWitt, had gone to Utah and there met a man named Shepherd with whom he became a partner. They were the first men to bring sheep to Utah. DeWitt became wealthy with several large herds. He settled in the Beaver, Utah, area. He brought another brother, Jim, and by the time Victor came, Jim also had large herds of sheep and was a leading citizen as president of the Bank and president of the School Board of Panguitch. Victor worked with the sheep and put all he earned back into sheep until he also had a large herd.

Feeling that his brothers DeWitt and Jim had most of the good sheep country sewed up in the southern part of the State, Victor decided to go to the Big Horn Basin in Lovell, Wyoming to start his sheep operation. After a few years, things were going well for him and his wife. They had six lovely children and the sheep business was prospering. There was only one problem. Dicey was a devout

Mormon and she was very desirous that Victor study the gospel and join the Church. The problem was that he'd been raised a Baptist and he vividly remembered the last words his mother uttered before he left for the West. "Dear Son, please don't be deceived by the Mormon religion. Although your brothers haven't joined their Church, both have married Mormon girls. While the girls seem nice enough, their children are being indoctrinated with those false beliefs. Remember, you're a Southern Baptist! If you want to be saved, stay with your religion. God bless and keep you!" This was the last time he saw his mother, for she died before he could again visit his home, but he could still see her earnest face and hear those last words she'd uttered to him.

Under Dicey's influence, Victor began to read the Book of Mormon. To his great surprise, he was convinced of its truthfulness. What should he do? He was in a great dilemma for he remembered his mother's words. Could he possibly be deceived and end up in hell? *One night he was praying fervently to know what to do. His wife was anxious for him to join the Church, but he still had all of those doubts. What if it was a hoax after all?*

He dozed off, still confused as to what to do. That night he had a dream. His mother seemed to be right in the room, anxious to get his attention. "Victor, we're waiting. We're waiting." Then she was gone. He awakened with great joy and assurance that he should join the LDS religion and have her temple work done. Gone were his doubts for what else could she be waiting for if not to have their temple work done. This proved to him that the Church was true.

Shortly after this dream, Victor was baptized and became an active member of the Church, much to Dicey's joy and his too. He later became a bishop in the Church, and of course, he had his parents sealed in the temple.

One cold winter morning, Victor was in bed with the flu and had been for several days. Dicey told him that she would make the fire that morning. She was rather new at building a fire, but had seen her husband throw a little oil or gas on the fire to start it. She did the same, and a great explosion took place. The room and Dicey were engulfed in flames in seconds. Victor heard the explosion, and jumped up and tried to enter the room but was unable to. He ran to the children's bedroom and got three of them out of the house and then tried to enter and get the other three and Dicey, but the flames drove him back. By then neighbors were watching the horrible scene. Victor was determined to go back in, but he was held back by neighbors and friends. The home was totally engulfed in flames by this time and entirely destroyed! As friends and neighbors tried to comfort Victor, he watched in anguish as his wife and three of their children died in the fire.

The horror and shock of this grisly scene nearly caused Victor to have a breakdown. He felt as though he was losing his mind. He could not find comfort in anything. He knew he had three children to care for, and he went through the motions of living, but he felt dead inside. The horror of watching helplessly while his dear wife and three of his children burned was more than he could bear. He was in a state of anguish all the time.

One night he was so agitated that he begged the Lord to give him peace of mind or take him. He knew that he must rest for he'd slept very little since the fire, and had felt awful guilt ever since the accident. "Oh, why didn't I get up and build that fire?" he'd exclaim to himself, yet in his heart, he knew that he'd been too ill to get up. That night Victor had a dream. A sweet, familiar voice awakened him, and there before him stood his wife, Dicey. She seemed calm and happy. "Victor," she said. "Promise you'll stop grieving for me and the children. We're fine, busy and happy, and waiting for you to finish your work on earth and join us. Take good care of our children there!" Then she was gone.

Suddenly all those feelings of anguish left him. A calm feeling of serenity and happiness filled his heart. Dicey said they were all well and happy. They were where nothing could hurt them again. He realized how selfish he'd been in thinking only of his loss. He knew that the children must be going through a bad time and needed his comfort and love and he must give it to them.

That morning he told the children of his dream. They were as happy as he was to know that their mother and brother and sisters were happy.

"That dream made all the difference in the world in our lives. It seemed as if a terrible load was lifted off our shoulders," Victor said.

Victor eventually married again and had two more sons and was active in the Church for the remainder of his life. *He knew that the Lord had answered his prayers in giving him the "peace of mind" he'd prayed for.*

The Gospel Transformed My Life

Connie Jordan was raised in a home where everything necessary was supplied, including a good education. The only thing that was missing in her life was any religious instruction. By hard study, she graduated with honors from a top university and then law school, but she always felt that something was lacking. Then she met the missionaries, heard the gospel and found life's true meaning. Then came a spiritual experience that would change her life.

I was born to parents who took good care of me, gave me a good education, and were loving and kind. However, I don't remember any religious teachings at all or ever attending church. In fact, the only time I remember hearing the name of God in our home was when my father occasionally cursed. I felt like a ship without a rudder as far as any knowledge of a loving Heavenly Father was concerned.

During my high school years, I made many mistakes because of this lack of knowledge. My main goal was to be popular, and the only way I felt I could accomplish this was to "follow the crowd." Later, as I saw many of my friends having great problems in their lives from using drugs and breaking the laws of chastity, I decided that wasn't the way to happiness, and I immersed myself in my studies. Fortunately, I learned easily and became a top student. I was accepted to UCLA and worked hard there, graduating with top grades. I was then accepted at Columbia Law School. During this time, my social life was rather meager. It seemed that even dating a fellow implied more than just having a good time, and something in me resented this. It made me feel cheap! After some time I met a young law student and we became great friends and had a good time together.

Many of my friends were having heavy relationships with their boy friends. They would become intimate with one person for awhile. Then their relationship would cool and they would find another. Because of this, many were having great emotional stress. I decided that I'd rather be single than be in such a relationship.

My family members were all present when I received my law degree. They were proud of me, and I heaved a sigh of relief. Even though I'd enjoyed school, the stress to keep my grade point up had been heavy, and I was eager to practice law.

I was soon hired by one of the best firms in our city. Because I was one of the rookies, I was given cases that no one else wanted. These were often messy divorce cases with children involved. My heart ached as I saw the children being used as pawns and torn between the parents.

As the years passed, my life settled down pleasantly and comfortably. I was able to find a nice condo in a good area, and I had many friends, both men and women, although no serious relationships developed. Money was no longer a problem. I felt secure as I was made a partner in my firm. I had decided that I would never find a mate, but regardless, my life was pleasant and enjoyable.

One cold, windy Saturday morning, I answered the door and there stood two young men. They said they were missionaries from The Church of Jesus Christ of Latter-day Saints, or Mormons. They seemed so young, clean and vulnerable to be out in the world that somehow they touched my heart and I invited them in. I offered them a hot cup of coffee. They explained that they didn't drink coffee, so I made them hot chocolate instead.

I'm an inquisitive person and had always been curious about the Mormons. That may have been part of the reason I was willing to listen to the young men that morning. The story they told interested me. I asked many questions, and young as they were, they were able to give answers that satisfied me. We talked many hours, and when they left, they gave me a *Book of Mormon* and another book, *A Marvelous Work and a Wonder*.

That night I'd planned to see a show with some friends, but somehow the missionaries had whetted my appetite to learn more about their church. I was anxious to read the books they'd left so I called and canceled our engagement and settled down with my books.

Some twelve or fourteen hours later, I had read more than half of the Book of Mormon. Being an attorney, I was constantly probing for truth and I knew that this book was no hoax. I slept for a few hours and then started on *A Marvelous Work and a Wonder,* and finished it that Sunday. I was shocked and stunned by all I'd read. Could this really be the true Gospel of Jesus Christ? My heart told me it was, but I'd now have to study it carefully since I'd only given it a cursory reading. I had more questions for the missionaries, so I called them. They'd just come home from church and they came right over. Again, they answered most of my questions, but they wanted me to meet and talk with their District President, President Hawkins. They assured me that he could answer any question I might have. They also invited me to attend church in the ward near me.

I attended the ward the next Sunday and was amazed at the large attendance. The people seemed to be so friendly and kind that I felt right at home. Relief Society was such a wonderful experience. I could see that it encompassed every facet of the sisters' lives. I also enjoyed the Sunday School class where they were studying the Book of Mormon. The teacher was a brilliant surgeon and the discussion outstanding. I was impressed, to say the least. Many of these people were extremely well-educated, and yet they all seemed to have a testimony that this was the Church of Jesus Christ.

The next day, the missionaries introduced me to President Hawkins. He was a fine man and also an attorney. I had a list of the questions that had been bothering me, and he answered them to my satisfaction. "Do you have any more questions, Sister?" he asked.

"No, I don't think so. Not at the moment, at least."

"May I make a suggestion to you. Read Moroni 10:4-5, and fast and pray about the truthfulness of this Church. The Holy Ghost will let you know of the truth of this great work."

I had done everything else, so I decided to take his suggestion. I now had a burning desire to know the truth, even though I knew that it would mean a complete change in my life if I accepted it. I'd had a strong nicotine addiction for many years, and although not an alcoholic, I drank wine with dinner and took a drink occasionally. The missionaries had told me that these things were not allowed because of the Word of Wisdom. I'd known for a long time that smoking was stupid.

It was a detriment to my health as well as a dirty, smelly habit. It was also expensive. Quitting was another thing. When the habit is ingrained deeply into your system, authorities say it is almost as hard to quit as it is to quit a heroin habit.

I decided to fast and pray about the Church on the coming Labor Day weekend. If I could get an answer, I'd tackle the smoking next. I fasted and prayed sincerely, but no answer came. As I finished my third day of fasting, I picked up the Book of Mormon and started to read. It seemed that I was right there with those ancient people. I could see them as well as I could see my friends when we were together. Then this strange feeling came over me, a sure knowledge that this book was true! I knew that Jesus is the Christ and that He is the Son of God and that this is His Church! I knew it as surely as anything I'd ever known. What joy filled my heart at that moment! I knew that I had a personal revelation, and to me, it was marvelous!

That evening, out of habit, I reached for a cigarette, and to my utter amazement, I didn't want it! All desire had left me. It seemed like a loathsome thing as I held it in my hand, so I threw all of my cigarettes away. To this day, I've never smoked nor have I wanted to. That desire seemed to have left me completely when I gained my testimony.

I called the missionaries and told them that I was ready to be baptized. Of course, they were delighted, but they asked me about my nicotine habit. I assured them that I had no desire to smoke and never would again.

I was baptized the next week. It was thrilling to me for my heart was filled with love and joy. I now realized why I'd always felt that something was missing in my life. It was a testimony of Jesus Christ. The realization that I was a child of God, and I had a Father I could talk to at any time. The gospel made me feel whole!

My friends didn't desert me, but as my friendships in the Church grew, I found that I had more in common with my LDS friends than I did with the non-Mormon friends, although I still love many of them dearly.

One day one of the new members in our firm came to me in a quandary. "I have a case that I must take in the morning. Would you take it? My mother is very ill, and I feel I must be with her." I inquired about the case and she said that it was one of the county cases we were forced to take occasionally. It seemed that this mother of a three-year-old had neglected her child. The mother was on drugs. The attorney had an appointment to bring the case before the judge the next morning. I found I could fit the case into my schedule so I told her to care for her mother and I would take her place in court.

The mother and child were brought into the courtroom by the social worker. The mother looked very "strung-out," the words one uses for a person who is on drugs. Then my attention turned to the child. Overlooking the tangled curls, the dirty face and hands, and the soiled clothing the child was wearing, it was plain to see she was a beautiful child though she looked thin and malnourished.

The judge berated the mother for neglecting her daughter, and told her that the child would be taken away from her, for this mother was a habitual drug user and not fit to care for a child. The mother was entered into a drug-treatment facility again although the judge told me privately that she had already been in several times and could not resist drugs when she got out. The judge talked to me, and it was decided that the child would be put into a foster home. Then the judge turned to the social worker. "Find a place for this child." she said.

"I've been trying to find a foster home for the child because I knew her mother couldn't care for her, but it seems that there isn't an opening right now. We'll just have to put her into juvenile detention," the social worker said.

"Oh, no," the judge said. "There would be no one to comfort her, and she'd be with older children. I only wish we had many more foster homes."

As I looked at the tiny child, my heart went out to her. Suddenly, I longed to bathe her, wash her lovely hair, and brush it and put her into clean clothes. I also wanted to give her some nourishing food. I couldn't believe my ears, but I heard myself saying almost against my will and against all common sense, "I'll take the child until you find a place for her."

The judge looked at me and smiled for the first time that morning. "Oh, that would be great. I surely hate to put her into detention."

They led the mother away in spite of the wails of the child. Suddenly I realized I was responsible for a small child who needed attention, and a sad and crying child at that. Who would tend her while I worked?

Suddenly I thought of my mother who was recently widowed. Perhaps she'd take her until I could make other arrangements. Today was my light day at work. I called and had my assistant take over while I carried a sobbing child out to the car. It seems that no matter how children are treated, they look upon their parents as security, and I knew that Kristen felt very forlorn when her mother left.

I had a chocolate bar in my car and I gave her a piece of it, which quieted her for a while. Then I took her home. I undressed the poor little waif, turned warm water into the tub and threw her clothes in the washer. They'd have to do until I could take her to the store for more.

She seemed to thoroughly enjoy the bath and even having her hair washed. I wrapped her in a warm robe while I brushed her hair, and waited for her clothes to dry. Then I sat her down to a bowl of warm, nourishing soup. The child ate like she'd been starved for days. I knew that I had done the right thing bringing her home.

Later, while Kristen was asleep, I called my mother. She agreed to keep her while I worked. I think she'd been lonely since the death of my father and needed something to do. Of course, this would be a temporary arrangement. The social worker was still looking for a family to take Kristen, but she hadn't found one.

Ever since joining the Church, I'd been anxious to receive my endowments in the temple. Finally the day came and I was sitting in the temple. *As I sat there that day, a voice said to me, "Adopt Kristen. She will be a blessing and a joy to you." I looked around to see if anyone else had heard the voice for it seemed so plain that I thought someone was talking out loud. I decided no one else had heard.*

My mind seemed to answer back, "But I can't. How can I take care of a child? I work, and she will be alone much of the time. My condo doesn't permit children. I would have to move. It's out of the question."

Again the voice said forcefully, "Adopt Kristen. She needs a home and you need her. You will be happy if you do." I started to argue with the unknown command again. "Perhaps her mother won't agree to the adoption. Drug addicts always feel that they'll get well and be able to care for their children."

The voice came again even more emphatically. "She will agree. Adopt Kristen!"

As I left the temple that evening, I felt happy but emotionally drained from the spiritual experience I'd just had. My mind was in a turmoil. I knew that the voice I had heard had come from the Lord. Could I just ignore such a command? As I picked up Kristen from Mother's home, she seemed genuinely happy to see me. I knew we were bonding. Yes, I would try to adopt the child. I couldn't refuse that command for I knew that if I did, I would be sorry. I believed in the Church. Then why not obey this command. This spiritual experience I had could not be ignored.

The next day I talked with the judge about adopting the child. She was delighted with my decision. She said she thought the mother would agree to give up the child since she had been hopelessly addicted to drugs for years. I could talk to her and try to get her to sign the necessary papers.

As I entered the Drug Rehabilitation Center, my heart was beating very fast. What if the woman refused to give up her child? The woman's name was Lola and I was taken to her room. I could tell that she was having a difficult time trying to master her addiction. She recognized me as her attorney in court. I told her that the social worker had been unable to place Kristen and that I had taken her temporarily. Now I wanted to adopt her. At first the mother refused to even consider the adoption. "I'll take care of my child as soon as I get out of here," she said.

"What will you do to support you and the child?" I asked. "Do you have an education, and can you find a good job?" She admitted that she didn't. "But I'll get trained to do something," she assured me.

"In the meantime, how will you take care of Kristen? What future will she have?"

Lola continued to tell me that things would work out for them. Feeling that I was up against a brick wall, I finally stood up to leave. "Here is my card. Call me if you change your mind. In the meantime, I'll take care of Kristen."

Weeks went by and I didn't hear from Lola. Meanwhile, I was becoming very fond of Kristen and she of me, and of my mother who tended her while I worked.

Lola was released from the detention center, but was not allowed to take Kristen until she'd proved her ability to stay off drugs. One day I received a call from the judge. Lola had been picked up for prostitution and was again on drugs. She was being held in jail and wanted to see me.

As I entered the jail cell where Lola was being held, I could see that she was in bad shape. Her eyes were bleary, her hands were shaking and she was emotionally distraught. "I must let you have my child," she blurted out. "I can't give her a decent life, hard as I try. I'm too hooked on these terrible drugs, and I'll do anything to get them. I'll sign the papers."

I hugged the signed papers to me as I returned home. Kristen was my child! The Lord knew that she needed me and I needed her. Adopting Krissie has meant some sacrifices in my life. I had to find a condominium where children were allowed. There were other problems of adjustment, but the blessings of having her outweigh the problems. She is a bright, beautiful child. We have a great relationship, and having her has surely given me something to live for. I thank God for sending her to me as I recall that night in the temple when I was directed by Him to adopt her.

Something new and wonderful besides Kristen has come into my life. I am now engaged to a wonderful man, a former mission president. I had begun to think that I'd never fall in love or marry, until I met this great man. He lost his wife some years ago, and felt that he'd never marry again, but we have fallen in love. He also loves Kristen, and she adores him. We plan to marry soon and be sealed together as an eternal family.

I am grateful to those two missionaries who called on me that day. Having the gospel of Jesus Christ, wonderful Krissie, and now my sweetheart in my life have made the difference as night from day. I now have a new and marvelous life to look forward to here and hereafter! What a blessing!

Alone

"Please God, don't let me die." That was the prayer Shirleen Jaussi breathed as she knew her plane was going to crash.

This is the amazing story of Shirleen Jaussi's miraculous survival from a plane crash. It tells of her five days and four nights alone and injured in the mountains before being found. This story has been made into a book and a movie called Solo *by Patricia O'Brien King and published by the Deseret Book Company. I wish to thank them for their kindness in letting me publish this short version of their book. I especially wanted to let Shirleen tell of the miracles that have come into her life as a result of this traumatic yet spiritual experience.*

Day One—Tuesday

The small plane taxied down the runway of the airport in Price, Utah, on June 23, 1981, and lifted gracefully into the clear summer sky. I was its only occupant. This gave me butterflies and a lonely feeling, for this was my solo flight which when completed, would give me my pilot's license. I couldn't believe that I, Shirleen Jaussi, would be a licensed pilot when I returned that day.

As I had quietly dressed for the flight that morning, I could not shake off a feeling of apprehension and dread. My five children still lay deep in sleep. Love welled up in my heart as I looked at them, and I had a difficult time leaving them and the comfort and safety of my home. Try as I might, I couldn't shake off that strong feeling of foreboding that almost overwhelmed me. I didn't want to make the flight that morning! "I wish I'd talked Craig out of this cross-country flight today. I just hate to be up in that plane alone. Why did I ever start this?" I said aloud.

This solo flight was the "big one," the flight I'd been preparing for so long, under the careful tutelage of Craig Humes, my instructor. He'd be at the airport now, I thought as I rushed toward the front door.

"Your glasses, get your glasses," a voice seemed to say, though I thought it a little silly for I'd only be gone a few hours and my contacts would work fine for that time. I hesitated, but I ran back and got my glasses. I'd be thankful later that I did.

I rushed to the airport. I didn't want to keep Craig waiting. He'd assured me that I was ready. We'd covered all the things I needed to know. "You have to go sometime, and you're ready," he assured me that morning as I told him of my feeling of reluctance. "All pilots get the jitters before their solo flight."

This was to be a three-legged course charted for Grand Junction, Colorado; Blanding, Utah; and then back to Price. Ten hours of solo flight were required before I could obtain my pilot's license.

Well, here I am up in the air alone, I thought. It was a lonely, and rather scary feeling.

As I flew to Grand Junction, I began to enjoy the trip. I was able to mark off my mapped checkpoints right on schedule. I called into the control tower and received the instructions I needed to find the airport. The wind had come up and it tossed the plane around some so the landing wasn't as smooth as I'd have liked.

The plane was soon refueled and I headed toward Blanding. As the plane neared the mountains, the Grand Junction tower announced that there was some turbulence in the area. In an instant, the turbulence I'd been warned about began tossing the plane around like a toy, then a huge down-draft dropped the plane to only 8,000 feet instead of the 8,500 where it should have been to fly over the mountains.

Just as I was recovering from the shock of the first down-draft, I felt another so powerful that I had no control over the plane. It seemed as if a gigantic force was pushing the plane toward the ground. Then I could feel the plane skimming the top of the trees. I remembered Craig's warning, "If you are going to crash, keep flying the plane as if you were going to land. That way you may walk away from it." With a horrible certainty, I knew that the plane was going to crash. *"Please, please God," I cried, "don't let me die."*

Suddenly there was a terrifying crash as the wing hit a tree and sheared it off. Then the small plane was flung wildly to the ground upside down between two pine trees.

I opened my eyes and sat there stunned for a minute. Then it all came back to me. The last thing I remembered was the plane coming down with a loud crash. I sat there in shocked amazement. I'd survived a plane wreck! *"I'm alive, I'm alive. Thank you, God, for letting me live," I cried over and over again.* Luckily the thick forest growth cushioned the fall and the bubble I was sitting in was still intact but upside down.

Gratitude filled my heart. I'd survived a plane crash! Then a thought suddenly struck me. Thirty-two gallons of gas had been pumped into the plane's tank fifteen minutes earlier. I had to get out as quickly as possible. The threat of an explosion filled me with terror. Before I left the plane I knew that I must see that the locator transmitter had been turned on, but my hands were so badly cut and were swelling so rapidly that I had difficulty as I fumbled with the antenna. I was finally able to turn it on.

Panic almost overcame me as I found I was locked inside the bubble. I was frantic until I found the catch and was able to pull the door open a little so that I could squeeze out. At that moment I was happy that I was a small person or I'd never have been able to squeeze through the tiny opening. I pulled my purse and jacket out with me and crawled out of the plane. Then I walked as fast as possible to a tree some twenty feet away. That was my last walk for more than six weeks.

At the foot of the tree I fell to my knees and began to pour out my gratitude to my Heavenly Father for his love and mercy in sparing my life. Then I fell into a sleep of utter exhaustion.

Excruciating pain in my right arm forced me awake. I can't stand this pain, I thought and flung my arm in a desperate attempt to relieve it. It snapped instantly into place for which I was thankful. Then I became aware of a terrific pain in my leg. I thought I'd pulled a muscle in my groin.

I began to check my other injuries. Blood was on my shirt, probably from a nosebleed. One knee was badly cut, and my stocking was glued to it with blood. One hand had begun to swell rapidly, and the other had three deep gashes that I was sure Jim, my physician husband, would have wanted to sew up. A fingernail had been ripped off—probably the most painful thing of all—and my wedding rings were smashed nearly flat. Blood and dirt had been ground into my face. I took tissues from my purse and began to clean myself up as well as I could.

A new fear possessed me as I realized that a strange set of halos began to form around my eyes. Fear of blindness gave away to an even greater concern—forest fire. I could both hear and smell the steady dripping of gasoline. I knew it would be impossible to stay ahead of a fire for I found I couldn't put any weight on my injured leg. Even crawling caused intense pain. I was panic-stricken for a few moments. The plane was still resting inertly in its upside-down position.

Nearly an hour had passed since the crash. It was now ten o'clock. I realized that I had at least two hours to wait before being rescued. My flight plan wasn't supposed to close until around noon. I kept thinking of the wonderful, warm bath I'd have, complete with marvelous-smelling bath crystals when I returned home and could clean off all the blood and dirt.

When Shirleen's plane was late, her husband, Jim, and Craig Humes were terribly worried and contacted the Civil Air Patrol. They assured them that they would do all in their power to help. The search began at once.

I now became aware of my new surroundings. They were fresh and lovely. Everything was lush and green and the place spilled over with wild flowers of many colors. There were quaking aspens and a few tall pines. Oak brush two or three feet high covered the ground. *How beautiful the world is,* I thought. How grateful I felt that the Lord had spared my life so that I could enjoy it. A few animals wandered by, probably in search of a watering trough, I thought. I wished I could walk so that I could find one as I now felt thirsty and dehydrated.

A helicopter sounded overhead. As the afternoon dragged on, four or five other planes flew over. I realized that they were probably looking for me. Why couldn't they see me?

I discovered an apple and seventeen sticks of gum in my purse. A can of soda pop was supposed to be kept in the plane at all times, but the last person to fly the plane had forgotten to replace it. I knew it was important to chew on something to keep my mouth from swelling so I unwrapped a stick of gum and put it in my mouth. How good it tasted.

The afternoon dragged by and darkness began to settle over my resting place in the forest. I had nothing to read so *I sang songs of thanks to Heavenly Father.* Oh, how I wished that I'd brought the small Book of Mormon that I usually carried in my purse. When the planes stopped coming, I realized that the search was over for the night, so I began making plans to sleep. I felt I would be warmer if I slept by the plane as my back would be protected, so I started dragging myself toward the plane, wincing at the pain that every movement caused.

As I settled down for the night, I again thanked the Lord for saving my life and asked for his protection during the night. At once a comforting peace settled over me. I realized, now, even more than ever before, how dependent we are on Him. I closed my eyes secure in the knowledge that I was being watched over by my Heavenly Father.

I slept fitfully, my thoughts often turning to my children and my husband and the fear that they must be feeling. I knew that I was only fifteen minutes out of Grand Junction. I kept trying mentally to communicate this to my husband. I was sure the search planes would find me in the morning.

The anxious group gathered at the Price airport knew that darkness would soon be settling in. Reluctantly they ended the search for that day. As Jim Jaussi headed home after the long day of fruitless search, he knew that he must face his children's questions. What would he tell them? He knew of the great possibility that their mother had been killed in the plane accident. He finally decided to tell the oldest child of that probability but not the younger ones. Jan, their oldest child was thirteen. As her father talked with her, she was almost overwhelmed with grief. Life would be unbearable without her mother, her best friend and confidant. The younger children found it hard to believe that their father couldn't find their mother. They wanted their mother and couldn't understand why she wasn't home.

Jim found it impossible to sleep as he wondered about Shirleen. Only two possibilities seemed likely. She was either dead or seriously injured and those injuries could cause her death. He pleaded with the Lord to care for Shirleen, protect her and keep her warm. "Please bring her back to me," he cried. "I barely have time to play a little with the kids and attend my Church duties. How will I ever find time to feed, bathe them and answer all their needs?" He had depended on Shirleen to take care of the daily needs of the family as his profession kept him extremely busy day and night for babies come at any hour.

The magnitude of the awesome responsibility of caring for the family alone was almost overwhelming and humbling. He pleaded for strength to face whatever was in store for him.

Jean Jaussi, Jim's mother, came from Lake Town, Utah to be with her son and his family. She shared the anxiety that her son was experiencing, and they prayed fervently that Shirleen would be found well, but their common sense told them that she was either seriously injured or dead in the crash. Although devastated at the thought of losing the woman he loved, Jim knew that he would have to accept the Lord's will, whatever it turned out to be. He was grateful that they had been good to each other and for the happiness they'd known, yet he wondered how he, and the children, could ever get along without her.

Day Two—Wednesday

As soon as it was light the next morning, Craig Humes and his wife, Deanna, met Jim Jaussi at the airport. They were all anxious to begin the search for Shirleen and the missing plane. Jim announced that he believed that Shirleen was only about fifteen minutes outside Grand Junction, but since the CAP was searching there and they wanted them to continue, they decided they would retrace Shirleen's flight looking for a clue.

Deanna flew with other searchers toward Blanding, while Craig and Jim headed toward Grand Junction. With them were two young men acting as spotters. Craig hoped that by flying the same route Shirleen had taken they might find her.

When I awakened Wednesday morning, the sun was already up. I began to realize just how painful my injuries were and how stiff and sore I was. Lying on the hard, rocky ground all night hadn't helped. I'd been awakened in the night by the penetrating cold. I was shivering so violently that pains began to shoot through my injured leg. What if I froze to death in that high altitude? I had painfully pulled myself over to the plane for I felt I would be warmer with the plane to my back. I also remembered window coverings there that might be a help in fighting the cold. I had removed a cardboard box containing a roll of black electrical tape. I used the tape to secure the window shades around my legs to keep out the cold, but even with the shades and the jacket I'd brought, I was terribly cold. In spite of the cold and the problems, I was grateful to be alive. Thankful too that I had run back in the house for my glasses. I would have felt helpless without them. My hands were so dirty now that it would have been difficult to insert the contact lens.

I realized that I was still in shock as I slipped in and out of sleep during the long day. I could do nothing but wait. In spite of the difficulties I was experiencing, *I was grateful to my Heavenly Father beyond belief that my body hadn't been seriously injured. I realized that my life had been spared by God's mercy. Love for God and his goodness filled my heart to overflowing!*

I knew that a search plane would be unable to see me in the forest where I was, unless it was directly over me. I could tell that the planes were coming from the direction of Grand Junction by my map. The landing upside down had disoriented me for awhile, but now I knew I was right in thinking Grand Junction was where I thought it was.

I placed my small, purse mirror on the silver fabric from the window shades from the plane as a reflector, hoping someone would see it. As I saw the commercial jets fly over, I imagined the passengers being served long, cold drinks. How I longed for one, but the only thing I had was a stick of gum which I chewed to keep my mouth from swelling.

Shirleen's instructor, Craig Humes, deeply regretted letting her go up in the plane alone. Had he let her go up alone too soon? Yet she had passed every test for readiness that he could give. He remembered Jim saying last night that they must make every effort to find her today for after that, the chances of finding her alive were slim. How could he stand it if she was killed? He knew that somehow he would feel responsible.

"Why did it have to happen in a plane?" he asked his wife that night.

"Maybe it was to get our attention, Craig. We will be the ones who will be most affected if she's been killed in the plane." Deanna was a member of the Church, but Craig was not. Since their marriage, she had slipped into Craig's life style and had gone further from those concepts which had been so important during her growing-up years.

That afternoon search planes were flying very close. If they flew a little closer, they would be just above me. It took about five minutes for a plane to go from the end of one grid to another. My excitement grew. I was going to be found. Then the planes no longer came back. I could tell that the search had been called off again because of approaching darkness.

Deep disappointment filled my heart, but I knew that I must get ready to spend another night alone. I'd promised myself that I wouldn't eat any of the apple until Wednesday night and since it was Wednesday night, I crawled slowly and painfully to the side of the plane, wrapped the plane's window coverings around me and took a bite from the precious apple. How delicious it tasted! I only allowed myself to eat half of it, savoring every mouthful to the fullest.

Shirleen's mother, Lola Hoskins, arrived in Price on Wednesday. She shared her fears and deep emotions with Jean Jaussi, Jim's mother. What will the family do without a mother? What will Jim do? They both wondered and agonized.

There was an almost overwhelming outpouring of love and concern for the Jaussi family. Jean Jaussi, Jim's mother, was kept busy answering the phone and the door and receiving food that friends brought.

Ward members had declared a fast for Shirleen on Wednesday. The Jaussi family were there even though they had been through much and it was hard to face more questions. The day had been long and hot, but as they thirsted, ward members remembered that Shirleen must have been without water all this time. Together the members of the ward knelt and offered up their heart-felt prayers for Shirleen's safety.

The Civil Air Patrol continued their search, coordinating the efforts of volunteers from three states—Utah, Colorado, and Arizona.

Day Three—Thursday

Craig Humes was again the pilot of the Cherokee, owned by the Jaussis and the Madsens. Ted Madsen was optimistic that they would find Shirleen this day, Thursday. Jim was visibly worried. He knew that Shirleen's situation grew more serious each hour. Even if she had survived death, she was now beginning her third day without water. She would also be very hungry.

Trying to spot the plane for a long day—ten or twelve hours—was difficult and very tiring in a small plane. As they flew toward Vernal to fly their assigned grids along with another plane piloted by a man named Ott Webb, Jim thought of what Webb had told him. He'd searched for CAP for forty years and had never found a survivor. He planned to retire soon, and he wanted desperately for this search to be successful.

I had spent an uncomfortable night. I had severe stomach cramps and pains as a result of eating the half of apple too fast when I'd not had food for so long. In spite of it all, I felt renewed hope this Thursday morning as I moved to my spot by the tree. Surely they would resume their search and fly over me today. As the planes moved further away, I was filled with despair and began to sob cries of loneliness and fatigue.

After my cry, I felt better and began to think of my wonderful children and my husband. How greatly I had been blessed! I found a small notebook and wrote each of them a letter, telling them of my love and appreciation for them. I also wrote a letter to my husband telling him of my love and my hope of being found, but what to do in case I wasn't found.

As I sat there thinking of the blessings the children had brought to our lives, I began to feel guilty. Jim wanted to have another child, but I had not wanted more babies. One of the conditions upon which I agreed to move from Salt Lake to Price was that Jim would stop talking about another child. *Suddenly I found myself telling my Heavenly Father that if I was found, I would gladly have another child that Jim seemed to want so much.*

Jim Jaussi sat in the cabin of the Cherokee. He thought it must be at least 100 degrees in there for he was bathed in perspiration. His thoughts turned to Shirleen. How could she possibly still be alive? If she was, she must be suffering from injuries. The thought of her being injured, suffering and lying in this terrible heat filled his heart with sorrow. He looked steadily at the earth, hoping for some glimmer of life or of the plane. He knew that he'd been criticized for allowing his wife to learn to fly. Their decision was a joint one. Shirleen was a capable woman with a mind of her own and she'd wanted to learn to fly as much as he had. They'd been concerned about Shirleen's mother living in Georgetown, Idaho. The decision to move from Salt Lake to Price to be with his friend, Lynn Dayton, in a large practice was still difficult because of the worry of being so far away from Shirleen's mother. That was when they decided that flying was the best solution. This decision was made after much prayer. His thoughts turned again to Shirleen. A cold hand seemed to touch his heart, for he knew that if Shirleen was still alive, her kidneys would stop functioning today or soon.

It was during these musings that Jim heard Ted's proposal that they do a ground search for Shirleen. "Just about everyone in Price has four-wheel drive vehicles. They could go over and look around the mountains near Grand Junction." Jim was worried about a large group of untrained people searching through rough terrain. They might have other victims.

At the Madsen home that night, a group had gathered. They were bent on a ground search. A man from the Search and Rescue Unit addressed the group. He told them that a ground search would be ridiculous. "We never look from the ground until we've spotted the victim from the air, and then it is sometimes difficult to find him."

It was then that Ted and Jim decided that they could not be responsible for inviting the whole community to search. They concluded that it would be best to make it an elder's quorum project with priesthood holders united in thought and purpose. The quorum was notified to be ready and wait for the final decision tomorrow afternoon.

Strangely enough, each day that passed brought me renewed strength. My biggest discomfort was the heat and the thirst, although some of my injuries continued to bother me. My thirst led me to suck the moisture from the stem of the grass-like weeds growing so profusely. I also sucked on a small piece of apple to get all the moisture out and continued to chew gum.

This Thursday night, I decided to find a more comfortable place than the rocky terrain beside the plane. I remembered a spot I'd found to keep out of the sun. There were lots of leaves. It seemed almost like a bed—probably the bed of a deer. I scooted painfully along the ground with my precious box and found the choice spot and settled down where I enjoyed a night of restful slumber.

Day Four—Friday

I awakened early Friday morning refreshed after a more comfortable night's sleep than I'd known since the wreck. As I began the torturous task of scooting my way toward the plane, I felt optimistic. I'd be found today!

As I looked toward the West from a different angle that Friday morning, the sun was shining in a huge area about one hundred and twenty-five yards away. I saw a large clearing I'd never seen before—

about twice the size of a football field. On one side it was bordered by a wire fence. It was like a revelation. I knew that I'd be seen there more easily.

"I've got to get there before the planes start searching," I thought. With almost feverish haste, I scooted laboriously along over the rough terrain as fast as possible. I found that pushing the box and then pulling myself up to it seemed less awkward. Painfully, I slowly made it to the clearing. Again my hopes were high. I'd be found today! Grateful that I'd made it to the clearing and full of hope, I sang one of my favorite songs, "I Am a Child of God," and waited to be rescued.

Jim, Ted, and Craig and Deanna Humes arrived in Grand Junction early that Friday morning. They knew that several planes were now flying over Grid 122. There was a sporadic ELT signal coming from that direction. In addition, a pilot had seen a flash from that direction yesterday (a flash from Shirleen's mirror), but had not been able to pick it up again. In addition to the planes, helicopters were preparing to fly early that morning. Usually a downed plane is found within twenty minutes of either its departure or arrival areas, so the section designated as grid 122 seemed the most logical spot for Shirleen's plane to have gone down.

Later in the day, when the group were sitting in the pilot's lounge, trying to analyze the available facts, the helicopters returned to Hill Force Air Base in Ogden with no news. This disappointed the group in the lounge. They'd been so sure that grid 122 was where the ground searchers should concentrate.

Jim finally agreed to a ground search and he and Ted decided that grid 122 was where the searchers should concentrate their efforts. When Jim contacted CAP officials he learned that the area had been searched thoroughly from the air and they were just about to give up on it and cross it off. Even the ELT signal had faded and it seemed hopeless.

"Do you care if we bring up some people to search on the ground," Jim asked. "Will we interfere with your search?" He was assured that it was all right.

Jim and his friends carefully mapped out grid 122. Each road was assigned a number and the map was divided into eight sections, each a twenty-five-square-mile area. They made copies of it for each of the vehicles that would be searching the next morning.

Most of the men planned to leave that evening and stay over in Grand Junction for the night. Only one motel room could be found for there was a convention going on, so most of the men headed for the KOA campground.

Jim met the group at the Church at six. He was determined that the group search should be as orderly as possible. He didn't want anyone to take any unnecessary chances. "Ward conference will be held on Sunday. I don't want anyone staying over to search after tomorrow night. We belong in ward conference. Our family will be in Church on Sunday and we'll go forward together."

Around eight o'clock Friday morning, as I sat by a quaking aspen at the edge of the clearing, I heard search planes coming. I frantically waved my makeshift flag and screamed at the planes that circled the clearing. I was full of thankfulness and relief in the thought that they'd seen me. Soon I'd be rescued! I knew that they'd send a helicopter for me and when I heard the whir of a chopper, I just knew it was coming for me. Much to my utter disappointment, the chopper disappeared and the sound faded away.

Later that morning, a yellow jeep pulled up at the edge of the trees on the opposite side of the clearing. They've sent the jeep to pick me up. Oh, how great. My heart sang. Again I waved and screamed, but after a few moments, the vehicle left. I just knew they didn't know how to get through a locked fence and would soon be back.

How the long hours dragged by as I waited, sure that I'd been seen and would be rescued, but no one came. Finally to get out of the dreadful heat, I scooted back in the trees. Why haven't the planes that flew right over me seen me, and why didn't the people in the jeep hear or see me, I kept wondering.

A horrible thirst almost overcame me. How I longed for another bite of apple or a cold drink. I felt that my throat was closing shut and I was having trouble swallowing. I found a tube of hand cream in my purse and licked the lotion, which felt very soothing. Then I settled down to wait. Oh how I wished for my little Book of Mormon to read that I usually carried in my purse.

As the sun went down and dusk began to settle in, I knew that I had to spend another night alone in the forest. This would be my fourth. What feelings filled my heart as I prepared for the lonely, dark night! I'd been sure that I had been seen and would be found that day. Feelings of loneliness and despair nearly overcame me, but my optimistic disposition took over, and I kept my spirits up by singing favorite spiritual songs, and thinking of my wonderful family. I just couldn't believe that after saving my life, my Heavenly Father would let me die out here alone from thirst and hunger. *After my prayers, peace filled my heart* as I curled up and slept twenty miles directly southwest of the KOA campground where the searchers were sleeping.

What a lovely dream I had. I thought that I was being visited by my Young Women's class. They found I was fine and promised to return and pick me up on their way back from the camp. Even the thunder and the lightning didn't bother me much for a gentle rain began to fall. I tried frantically to catch some of the drops in my mouth, but only succeeded in getting a few.

Day Five—Saturday

On Saturday, which was to be the fifth and final day of the search, Jim met Craig, Deanna Humes and Ted Madsen at the airport. There was a different mood about the search today. Jim expressed his great appreciation to the Humes for their loyal support during this trying time and for Ted's support and help. By the time their plane reached Grand Junction at seven o'clock, the twenty-four men from the Church were at the airport eagerly awaiting their assignments.

Each vehicle and person was assigned a number to correspond to the area into which grid 122 had been divided. "We want you to come back here and sign out before heading home. Everyone must be back by 6:00 pm. If anyone is out past 6:30, we're coming in after you." Jim reminded them again that they were to take no chances, but were to stay near the road and their vehicles. Then he added, "The chance of finding Shirleen alive is nearly impossible and even the odds of finding her body are slim. All the armies in the world couldn't find Shirleen if she's not supposed to be found, but if she is, this group right here can do it." The group left in a solemn mood, anxious to put forth every effort to find the missing Shirleen.

A few miles away, I crawled out to the clearing. Many thoughts filled my mind. Would I be found today, Saturday, the fifth day I'd been alone? If not, how much longer could I last? I was desperately homesick for my husband and children and lonesome for the sound of a human voice. Oh, why couldn't they find me? I thought of the two coyotes I'd heard fighting savagely on the other side of the clearing during the early morning hours. The noise had continued for hours, it seemed. Finally when it stopped, I felt that one of the animals was dead.

The planes came at just about the same time they'd come other days. I waved my flag wildly and yelled as they began circling the clearing. One pilot seemed to look directly at me so I waved and smiled. I just knew he'd seen me and help would come soon.

As they started their search that Saturday morning, Jim, Deanna Humes and Ted Madsen all knew that this day there was a different feeling for they all knew that this was the final day of the search.

Jim, Brent Johnson and Ted Madsen headed for their assigned area in Jim's suburban. They wanted to check out some mountains and a deep canyon south and east of Grand Junction. After they'd been searching for awhile, Brent said, "Jim, obviously you think Shirleen is not alive." Brent could see that it was difficult for Jim to answer.

"Medically it's impossible for her to still be alive," Jim said quietly. "Perhaps it's a kindness if she is dead. If she was hurt badly enough to be unable to reach help, she would be suffering immensely. I don't want that." He went on to say that he and her mother wanted to find her body. He couldn't stand the thought of leaving her out here.

Gardell Grundvig, Lynn Lemon, and John Edison seemed to find problems even getting out of Grand Junction. Not only was it hard to find where they were supposed to go but how to get there. Thirty minutes later, they were still driving around Grand Junction, crossing and re-crossing river bridges and feeling totally confused. Finally, at about nine o'clock, they found the road toward their area. They had diagramed on the map what their general approach would be. Starting at one corner of their small grid, they planned to move across and down to the corner and working through the middle and back across the same way. The first few roads they tried had No Trespassing *signs posted with locks on them. Finally they found an accessible road, but soon they found it would be impossible to drive on. Crevices five feet deep blocked their way. Once again they searched for an access to their area. No road was available. They seemed to be blocked at every turn with either a dead end or locked gate.*

"We've wasted enough time. We must get on the right course," Gardell said. "Let's pray again for help and direction."

The three men climbed back into the truck and prayed to Heavenly Father for direction in their search. Then they drove up a dirt road, coming again to a locked gate. There was a path along the fence, so they drove along the fence to see if they could find another opening. A moment later, they saw something off in the trees.

What joy and gratitude filled my heart as I realized that I'd actually been found and was going home. How can I ever describe my feelings as the blue truck came to the same place where I'd seen the yellow truck the day before? Someone's coming, I thought, stand up, stand up. The pain was intense, but I didn't care. I just knew I had to stand up! I leaned against the tree for support, waved and called and miraculously they'd heard and came to my rescue! Thank You, Heavenly Father!

"Are those cows?" Gardell asked.

"Looks like a couple of cows and a bull," John answered.

"Look, there's a sheepherder," Lynn joined in. "Let's ask her if she's got a key to the gate."

John, who was nearest the window thought he heard a woman call out, "Please help me." He turned to the others, "I think I hear a voice; hey, what do we do?"

"Let's ask her if she's got the key to the gate," Lynn suggested.

They climbed out of the truck and called back, "Can we help you?"

"Yes, my leg's hurt. I can't walk."

The three men jumped the fence and headed toward the woman. Soon a shocked John who was in the lead called back, "Hey, I think this is Shirleen. It is Shirleen!"

The men rushed toward me. "You're alive, You're alive," they all exclaimed joyfully as they hugged me.

It is difficult to imagine how overjoyed and grateful I was at the sight of the first human beings I'd seen in five days. I laughed and exclaimed, "I can't believe I've been found, and by people I know! Have you guys got any water? I'm so thirsty!"

Lynn leaped back through the brush after the thermos, and John Gardell said, "Here, Shirleen, put your arms around our necks and we'll help you back to the truck."

"Oh, please carry me, just carry me. I'm so dirty and I know I smell terrible, but please carry me."

"No lady, you're not dirty, you're beautiful," John said.

Lynn came with the thermos and began pouring water down my throat.

The three men couldn't take their eyes off me, touching my hands or trying to make me comfortable. I guess I still looked pretty good in spite of the ordeal I'd been through. Although my makeup had long faded, my wedge-cut hairdo still fell obediently into place. My pants and velour shirt didn't have a single rip, only a few drops of blood, and my shoes were intact. I knew I looked a bit wan, but actually I guess I looked pretty good for what I'd been though.

While Lynn and Gardell made me comfortable on the mattress in the back of the truck, John got on his CB radio to inform everyone of the marvelous news. No one answered so they raced the car toward the general store they'd seen a few miles back .

"You're going too fast. I'd hate to think I'd lived through a plane crash only to die on the road now," I said.

Within minutes the truck pulled in at the store. Gardell and John ran inside to call the airport, while Lynn used the phone outside to call the sheriff. He told him to inform the men the search was over. Then he yelled, "Shirleen, what's your home phone number?" The line was busy so he called his own home, wanting to get the news to the family as fast as possible.

Susan Lemon had been trying all day to get away from the house to do some errands, but she hadn't made it yet. When Lynn called, she knew why. When she heard Lynn yelling, "Shirleen's okay! She's alive! Run over and tell her family." She drove over as fast as she dared, honking her horn as soon as she turned the corner of Apple Circle.

When Lynn told me that our line was busy, I gave him Jim's private, unlisted number, and he dialed that. The operator said to Jean Jaussi,

"I have a collect call from Lynn Lemon and Shirleen Jaussi." Jean misunderstood and answered sadly, "Shirleen Jaussi is not here."

"No," Lynn said, "You don't understand. It's not for Shirleen, it's from Shirleen."

Almost at that moment, Susan Lemon arrived at the Jaussi home and began pounding on the door. People gathered from all over the house as she shouted out the good news.

Sheer joy and confusion filled the house. Jean, still on the phone yelled above the confusion, "I can't believe it. Is it really true?"

Lynn carried me to the phone booth and I talked to my joyous family, one by one. My mother said that hearing my voice and knowing I would be fine was the greatest news she'd had since I was born.

Lynn looked on with satisfaction. *All week Lynn and his wife had been impressed that I was alive. Susan had seen me alive and well in a dream, and Lynn had seen me leaning against a tree as he prayed for me.*

When I hung up the phone the tears of sorrow that had been shed in the Jaussi home had turned to tears of joy and thanksgiving. The children painted messages of welcome all over the street and others tied yellow ribbons on every tree in the neighborhood.

The sheriff pulled in just ahead of the ambulance. He walked past as I sat on the end-gate of the truck, sipping Sunny Delight with water. "Where's the victim?" he asked.

"I'm the one," I piped up.

"You're the victim?" he asked incredulously.

I hadn't wanted to ride in the ambulance, but the sheriff told me I had no other choice. I finally agreed, but insisted that a friend ride with me. I'd been alone long enough.

After a hot, forty-five-minute ride to St. Mary's Hospital, I was whisked inside. Although I was embarrassed by the fact that I had not been able to keep clean, I was assured that I'd be clean and lovely by the time my husband and family arrived.

A doctor examined me to determine the extent of my injuries. He found a broken pelvis, fractured in two places, but my cuts were healing nicely.

Although I resisted, the doctor started an IV on me. He was equally insistent. "Do you think I'm going to let you die here in the emergency room after surviving for five days in the mountains? You have no idea how unstable you are."

On their way back to Grand Junction, Jim, Brent, and Ted had stopped to check out a couple more canyons. By the time they arrived at Monarch Aviation it was 6:15 p.m. To their surprise, none of the four-wheel vehicles was here.

"Looks as if they've all come and gone home already." Jim felt a sense of abandonment. As they climbed wearily up the stairs to the pilots' lounge they found it deserted. Jim and Ted went over to the wall maps while Brent found the sign-out board and began checking to see if everyone was accounted for. Suddenly he yelled, "Look at this!" Russ Wilson had written on the sign-out sheet, "Shirleen is found—go to St. Mary's Hospital!"

An explosion seemed to shake the room. All the men were pounding on each other's backs, jumping up and down, hugging each other and yelling at the same time.

Jim, the strong one, started to cry. Then suddenly he stopped. "That's a terrible joke for someone to play on me. Why would anyone do this?"

"Russ Wilson would never do this," Ted answered.

On the way to the car, they paused briefly and offered a prayer of thankfulness and gratitude.

"Where's St. Mary's hospital?" Ted asked.

Jim answered, "I think it's in Salt Lake."

As they rushed down the stairs, Jim asked someone passing by, "Have you heard about it? Who found her?"

"A church group from Price," came the response.

Jim began to cry again. "The Priesthood—the Priesthood found her!"

Jim was in such a state of shock that his friends had to help him into the Suburban. For him, Shirleen had really come back from the dead.

Someone remembered that there was a St. Mary's hospital in Grand Junction and asked directions from a passerby and they rushed to the hospital.

Every searcher stayed at the hospital. They not only wanted to look at me to be sure I was real, but they also wanted to see the priceless moment when Jim and I met again.

Jim ran into the hospital and met Lynn. "Who found her?" he cried. "We did." Lynn replied. Jim wrapped his arms around him and hugged him.

Lynn led Jim down the hall to my room for the great meeting. I wasn't there. I'd been wheeled down the hall to the phone for an interview with the International Press from New York.

I looked up to see Jim rushing down the hall. I handed the phone to Brent. Neither Jim nor I could find words to express our deep feelings. Jim tenderly took my hands in his and kissed them and then gazed into my eyes. His look told me of the joy and happiness he felt, and the same feelings filled my heart.

Epilogue

As the entire ward met at ward conference that Saturday evening, there was a joyous feeling in the air as the congregation sang, "Now Let Us Rejoice." The bishop announced that after the closing prayer by Brent Zollinger, one of the Jaussi family's home teachers, they would all adjourn to the airport. The feeling of excitement in the air was almost palpable as the large crowd watched the Cherokee touch down on the runway and taxi around. The door finally opened and Shirleen appeared. At that moment the crowd joined in a song Shirleen loved, "I Am a Child of God." Everyone there knew they had just witnessed a miracle.

Shirleen's Thoughts Sixteen Years Later

As I look back on that traumatic and miraculous experience, I realize that it has enriched both my life and the life of my family immeasurably.

My husband had long wanted another child but I had resisted, saying that five children were enough. Now I was ready to do the Lord's will, and our precious daughter, Julie, was born exactly one year to the day after I was found near the wreckage of my downed plane. I also had another wonderful child, Joshua, that I would never have had but for this humbling experience. What great blessings these two children have added to our lives!

My flight instructor, Craig Humes, and his wife Deanna have become active in the Church because of this experience. This makes me very grateful, for they are wonderful people and our great friends, and I'm sure that the Lord is very pleased. We have also heard from other people who have had their testimonies strengthened because of my experience, and every member of our ward feels a greater love and appreciation and closeness for each other.

I have an even deeper appreciation and love for my great husband and wonderful children because of this experience. Each day is precious when I think of how I nearly lost my life and was blessed to have more time on the earth to enjoy my great blessings.

Would I go through that harrowing experience again? Yes, I would, hard as it was, for my blessings far outweigh the suffering I experienced. I am better, stronger, and a more humble, grateful person because of this and my family is also. *I praise God every day for His goodness in saving my life, and I say this in the name of Jesus Christ, Amen.*

Don't Talk Religion to Me

Mark Haley, according to his own words, was an infidel. By the patience and love of his home teachers over a period of several years, he finally became active in the Church. Through this conversion, he was able to conquer terrible habits of addiction and find happiness with his wife and with life that he had thought impossible.

My father had been baptized a Mormon but never was active. Mother was converted, but never really became active either. As a result, the Church was not important in my life. Looking back, my parents were good people, but they liked to socialize and party too much to make the gospel part of their life.

I don't remember when I first started tampering with cigarettes. My father smoked, and I must have "borrowed" a few from him. I guess I was about fourteen. Anyway, the habit became as deeply ingrained in me as it was in him. Drinking goes along with smoking, and I started to drink, mainly as a recreational thing at first. When my first marriage failed, I became very depressed and started to drink more heavily. It seemed to be the only way I could cope with my problems, or so I thought. I didn't realize that I was only compounding them. Along with drinking goes cursing. I heard plenty of that where I worked, but I can't blame anyone else for my bad habits. A friend told me later that she dreaded to even talk to me on the phone because of my cursing. It was such a habit with me that I didn't even know when I did it.

I finally met a beautiful and good woman, Meg. Her marriage had failed also, so we had a lot in common. After we were married, she proved to be as lovely as she looked and a good home-maker. As I said,

I knew very little about the LDS Church although I'd been around Mormons all my life. One thing I knew was that alcohol and tobacco were against the Word of Wisdom, and since I was deeply involved with my cigarette habit and loved beer, I didn't want to give these vices up nor did I want anyone preaching to me about my bad habits or anything else! No one could tell me anything! Meg was not LDS, but she was a spiritual woman with a firm belief in God.

One day an acquaintance, Jim Burton, called and said that he was our home teacher and asked if he and his home teaching companion could visit us. I told him to come if he wanted to, but not to discuss religion for I simply wasn't interested.

Jim and his companion came while I was watching the sports channel. They asked if they could watch it with us. They knew I was interested in sports.

We had such a pleasant time together that we asked them back, and it soon became a habit to watch games together. Often, Jim's companion was unavailable and then he'd bring his lovely wife, June. We became such fast friends that we started to take treks into the mountains together and spend a lot of time with them. Eventually, they became our closest friends. It seemed so refreshing to be around people who never swore, smoked or drank. Even though they never criticized me in the least for my bad habits, I began to feel ashamed and guilty when I swore or smoked, and I tried to stop. We realized that these were high-quality people. This friendship went on for several years. During this time, they never tried to talk religion to us, but were merely great examples. Finally one day I called Jim and asked, "Why don't you ever talk about your Church to us? Meg has always been rather curious about the Mormons."

"I didn't talk about religion because you told me not to," Jim said.

"Well, I think Meg is ready to learn something about the Church by this time. You may give us the lessons if you like," I said, lamely. I, too, was ready to hear more about the gospel, but ashamed to admit it after what I'd told Jim when he first called.

Meg wanted to compare the Mormon Church with what she was taught as a child in the Baptist Church so she bought a Book of Mormon and had been reading it. I, too, had read some in it, and was amazed at what I read. It rang true.

When they came again, Jim asked Meg how she liked the Book of Mormon. "I think it's great!" she replied. "I'd like to really study it. I went to a Baptist church some as a child and young woman, but after my divorce, I was usually working on Sundays and lost all contact with a church. Now we have plenty of time, and I think we should study the scriptures and become active in a church."

Jim gave us a fine lesson on the importance of keeping the Sabbath Day holy, and then said, "Meg, I think it would be well to call in the missionaries. I believe they will be better able to teach you than I am. Would you like that?"

Meg agreed, and we were soon taking the discussions. The missionaries were two young boys who really knew the gospel. They were so enthusiastic and helpful that we soon came to love them.

As we read and studied the Book of Mormon and discussed it with the missionaries and Jim, a different spirit seemed to possess me. Eventually, I prayed to know whether the Book of Mormon was true, and one day, to my surprise, I knew without a doubt of its truthfulness. The spirit of rebellion had left me. I wanted to be active in the Church, but I knew that first I must master those addictive habits I'd acquired. I knew that smoking was terrible for my health, but I'd tried to quit many times and had given it up as utterly impossible. I'd played cards with a group of men for years. While we were playing we'd smoke and drink beer, so by the time I got home, I was almost drunk. I knew that this didn't do me any good either, but I didn't seem to be able to quit. *Now I prayed humbly every day that those terrible vices that I felt I couldn't do without would become repulsive to me, and that the desire for them would leave me. I also stopped joining my friends in their card games for they were drinking and smoking. I reasoned that being around those things that I was addicted to would only heighten my desire to use them.*

What a terrible struggle I had. Satan really knows how to bind us to him, for he takes away our free agency and makes us his. I'd go without for awhile and then, in a weak moment, I'd succumb. *All this time I was praying fervently to be released from this terrible addiction.*

I kept a package of cigarettes on my night stand just in case I couldn't resist a smoke and might spend a sleepless night walking the floor. One morning I woke up and out of habit reached for a cigarette, but those cigarettes actually looked so repulsive to me that I couldn't wait to throw them into the garbage. The same was true of beer. I had lost all desire for it. How joyful and free I felt! I knew a great load had been lifted from my shoulders, and my prayers had been answered. Our home smelled so strongly of cigarette smoke that it was nauseating to us, so we had it scrubbed and repainted. We also had new carpet installed. Now the smell of nicotine in the car bothered me to the point that I finally sold it and bought a new, clean-smelling one.

The great thrill of my life came when Meg was baptized. I knew she'd be a great member and that someday we'd be able to be married in the temple for time and all eternity.

About this time, a friend asked us if we would like to go to one of the Institute classes held every week. We found that they have great teachers for these classes. They teach the college students religion. Meg and I attended and found that the classes were marvelous. They lasted an hour and a half, and we had time to study the gospel in depth. Here we really learned the gospel.

I formerly had a very negative attitude toward everything. I now endeavor to live a more Christ-like life. A friend asked me why I was living the gospel so strictly and I told him that I'd wasted so much time living the wrong way that I wanted to make up for lost time. One man who'd been inactive for years was asked why he'd become active in the Church and he said, "I'm cramming for the finals."

We've had several callings in the Church since becoming active. I've worked with the Boy Scouts, been president of the Young Men's and been a stake missionary, a calling that I began with fear and trembling but later came to love. With the Lord's help, we've been successful in activating several couples.

Currently, Meg is in the stake Relief Society presidency, and I'm the teacher of the Gospel Doctrine class. If you really want to learn the gospel, teach that class. I appreciate the fact that I must study diligently in order to teach it, and I know I've grown in that calling.

Our temple marriage was a glorious experience. It is difficult to explain the joy I feel now in comparison to my life before I became active in the Church. I truly feel as if I'd been reborn. I now have something to live for and to look forward to in the next life.

I thank my Home Teacher, Jim, with all my heart for his patience in sticking with me! Without Jim and his wife's kindness and love, I'd never have become active, and Meg would never have joined the Church!

I know for a surety that the Gospel of Jesus Christ is true, that Christ lives and is the head of this Church, and I say these things in the name of Jesus Christ.

Unconditional Love

Two great forces were working in the conversion of Jeremy Warburton. First was the love his father expressed to him instead of the criticism he expected. The other was the power of a great teacher in the lives of his students as this letter, written by Brother Jeremy to his institute teacher, Brother Robert Wahlquist, attests.

Brother Wahlquist is a master teacher who taught religion to the college students in Vernal, Utah, and to one adult class. His classes were overflowing and his message so powerful that one could not attend without gaining a firm testimony and being renewed and strengthened in the gospel.

Dear Brother Wahlquist:

I would like to thank you for your powerful testimony of Jesus Christ, and I would like to bear my testimony that your Institute class has changed my life.

About seven years ago, I began using drugs and alcohol. During the past three years, I became a heavy drug user, despite coming from a strong LDS family. I told people I was no longer a member of the Church.

Last October I was arrested with drugs. Part of my sentencing included going to *Narcotics Anonymous,* or attending your Institute class. At first I attended with the wrong attitude, and I still drank frequently. Last May I was drinking and was arrested for violating my probation and even charged with crimes I didn't commit.

While in jail, I decided to get bailed out and then run from the law, but my dad visited me and told me that despite everything I had done, he loved me. I returned to my cell in tears. When I got there, I noticed a Book of Mormon that just happened to be there. Over the next two days, I read more than half the book.

My dad bailed me out. A couple of days later, I attended your class for the first time with the right attitude and I felt an amazing spirit, especially when you bore your testimony. Since that time, I've read the Book of Mormon twice, the Doctrine and Covenants, *The Miracle of Forgiveness,* and I'm currently reading *Jesus the Christ.*

I have taken the sacrament for the first time in three years and I have also completed outpatient drug rehabilitation. Most importantly, your class has helped me gain a testimony of Jesus Christ. It has helped me learn to turn to the Lord in time of need, and has shown me how to use the scriptures in my daily life.

Even though you have a very busy life with so many students, and many duties as a bishop, you've always taken the time to help me. I promise to take your class more than my probation requires, and will try to get others to attend this great program. Thanks again for giving me back my life!

Thank you,
Jeremy Warburton

Better Than a Steak Dinner

Brother Wahlquist was the Institute teacher in Vernal, Utah. He taught the college students and one class of adults. I had heard what a powerful teacher he was, but was not prepared for just how powerful his teaching was until I began taking his class. The seminary building was literally packed with people. He kept us on the edge of our seats. Usually when I've attended such a class, the enrollment dwindles down as time goes by, but not in this case. It increased to the point that he had to bring in a whole new row of seats. How fortunate we were to have such a great teacher for our young people! I don't feel that anyone could come away from his class without a strong testimony.

The Church of Jesus Christ of Latter-day Saints is true. I believe that I have always known that it is true. From the time I was a young child, I recognized the Lord's hand in my life and felt him answering my prayers. Some individuals have marvelous conversion stories to tell when they finally find the gospel—whether they are finding it for the first time or after a long absence from the Church. Such experiences are sacred, personal and spiritual in nature. A wise individual would only share such experiences as inspired by the Spirit and only for the edification of others.

With this fact in mind, I must admit that I was hesitant to give my testimony to Sister Washburn for this book. Finally, after reading a collection of experiences from others, including *EFY* books and experiences from Church magazines, I have felt the Lord would approve sharing some observations from my life and some general ways that I have seen the Lord answer prayers.

While I have always known the Church is true, during my early years I continued to lean on my wonderful father's testimony and the testimony of my seminary teacher, Brother Thomas. It was through my seminary experience that I finally gained a testimony and could stand on my own. We were studying the Book of Mormon that year. I had been reading off and on during the fall, not really being that serious about daily reading. Finally, Christine, a friend of mine, and I decided we would have a race to see who could finish the Book of Mormon first. The loser would take the winner out for a steak dinner.

Each day we checked each other's progress. It was a very exciting few weeks. When one surged ahead, the other made the time to read many pages and catch up. Finally, one Saturday night with Christine starting Moroni and I just starting Ether, we knew someone would win tomorrow. There was a stake youth dance that night, and we watched each other like hawks to insure that neither one sneaked off to finish reading during the dance. Anticipation was high. Excitement was in the air. Not so much for finishing the Book of Mormon, but for winning.

Yet the Lord had other plans. After the dance, I was much too tired to read and so I set the alarm clock for early Sunday morning. I intended to win! As the sun shed its first light on that chilly fall Sabbath day, it found me well into the Book of Ether. As I read page after page of the rise and fall of the Jaredites, my heart and mind began to feel a subtle change. I could almost see the Brother of Jared seeing the finger of the Lord. I could almost hear the sounds of battle as Shiz and Coriantumr engaged in the final struggles for supremacy.

As I read Moroni's faithful words in Ether 15:34, the phone rang. I can't really explain what happened during the next few moments. I was pounded by a myriad of emotions simultaneously. The euphoria I had been feeling as I read was broken. It was like I was coming out of a beautiful dream. I knew the phone would be for me. I knew it would be Christine telling me she was finished. I felt disappointment, sadness, frustration, and relief all mixed together. I jumped out of bed and headed to the hall to answer the phone. To my total amazement, it wasn't for me. It wasn't Christine. Would I have finished the Book of Mormon that day? Would what happened next have happened anyway another time? Would I have gained the testimony I did in some other way? As I was to learn later, the hand of the Lord was playing an essential role in my life.

I turned back to my room and to the Book of Mormon with renewed determination to finish. I sped through Moroni one, then two, then three, four, five, and six. As I read Moroni seven, subconsciously I began to notice a theme. "Ask the Father in my name . . ." (Moroni 7:26). "Pray unto the Father with all the energy of heart . . ." (Moroni 7:48). "Continually praying unto God the Father in the name of his Holy child . . ." (Moroni 8:3). "Pray for them, my son. . . ." (Moroni 8:28). "I pray unto God that he will spare my life . . ." (Moroni 9:22). "I would exhort you that ye would ask God . . ." (Moroni 10:4).

As I finished Moroni 10:34, I jumped from my bed to run and call Christine. I had won! I had finished first! The steak dinner was mine! But as I tried to go through the door of my room I heard a voice say two words. I don't know if the voice was an audible voice, the voice of the spirit, or just a thought that came so strongly into my mind, but I do know that it was from God. The two words were just as clear as could be: "TEST IT!"

I then knew what my subconscious had been noticing. Pray . . . Ask God . . . Kneel . . . Without another thought of the contest, the steak dinner, or Christine, I turned back and knelt by my bed. I wanted to know if the Book of Mormon was true more than I wanted to know anything in my entire life. "Test it." Test Moroni's promise. Ask God if it is true!

With the faith of a child, which I was, I pled with my Heavenly Father to answer my plea. I can't or won't describe what happened next. I cannot describe the smallest part of what I felt at that time. Suffice it to say, I knew the Book of Mormon was true. I knew God lived. I knew God answered prayers. I knew The Church of Jesus Christ of Latter-day Saints was true!!!

I came to know these things for myself. There would be no more leaning on others for a testimony. I now had my own testimony. I rejoice in the beauty of what the Lord gave me at that time. My testimony of the Book of Mormon is very sacred to me. I hold it very dear to my heart. I thank the Lord that when the phone rang it was not for me. I had gained something far more lasting and exceedingly more valuable than a steak dinner.

Oh, about the steak dinner. I won, although I never collected. Christine had also set her alarm for early Sunday morning, but one thing and another had interrupted her and by the time I saw her at Church later that same day, she still had not been able to find the time to finish. Truly the Lord was watching out for one of his children. I will love Him forever for the experience of that day!

You Will Be Compensated

Mina and Lynn Murdock were stalwart members of the LDS Church all their lives. The loss of their young son was a devastating blow to them, but they were comforted by the promises of a priesthood blessing and saw the fulfillment of it in their lives.

Mina, and her husband, Lynn N. Murdock, had two young boys, ages seven and five years old. The older boy, Clair, had many bouts with tonsillitis so his parents decided to have his tonsils out on the advice of the doctor. The younger boy, Donnie, didn't have the same trouble, but in those days, nearly sixty years ago, tonsils were often taken out as a precaution, so it was decided that they would take his out at the same time.

The two boys were given a priesthood blessing on the morning of the operation and Mina took them to the doctor's office where the operation was to be performed. "I want to go first," Donnie said. He was helped onto the operating table and the office girl began to administer the ether.

A short time later Mina called her sister to come to the office. She said, "Donnie can't take the ether. Something is wrong and Dr. Eskelson has called Dr. Hansen." Both doctors worked feverishly with the child for a long time before they told Mina that he was dead. She simply couldn't believe this horrible news. What a terrible shock to her and her husband! The thought that she'd taken a perfectly healthy child to have his tonsils out and he'd died on the operating table before the operation even began was unthinkable to her. We all felt it was from an overdose of ether since the office girl had little training.

Mina mourned for Donnie and could not be comforted. Lynn was in the Stake Presidency so he and the stake president gave Mina a blessing. In it she was told that Donnie was fine. He was in the celestial kingdom, and she would be compensated many times over for her loss. A feeling of sweet, calm peace settled over Mina, and she was able to get on with her life. All agitation left her.

A couple of years later a baby girl, Linda, was born to the Murdocks. Then later another girl, Luann. The girls and Clair brought her happiness for they were all fine children and stalwart in the gospel. Linda married a returned missionary and they became the parents of six boys. All six of those boys were excellent students and all filled missions. Those fine boys fulfilled the promise in that blessing, but the Lord had other blessings for the faithful couple.

The second daughter, Luann, received her degree and teaches business in a high school. She and her husband, Dennis, have four lovely girls who had made Mina very happy.

Their son, Clair, became a Commander in the Navy. He married a wonderful woman, Doris, whom Mina and Lynn loved. They had six fine talented children, so the Lord more than fulfilled his promise made in the blessing.

Mina served as a teacher to the young missionary-age youth in her ward and saw most of her class fill missions. She gave each one a leather-bound copy of the scriptures. Lynn served as Bishop, was in the stake presidency, and both he and Mina served in the Salt Lake Temple for about thirty years.

Mina died at the age of eighty-four after a life devoted to the Church, and Lynn was buried a year from the day of her funeral. A few days earlier as we visited he was fine, but he told us he was lonely for Mina. He fell on the stairs of their condo and never regained consciousness.

In spite of the loss of their son, the Murdocks were well compensated for their loss, and they are now with the fine son they lost for only a little while.

Testimonies of Two Sister Missionaries

We are privileged to have two lovely, lady missionaries presently serving in Vernal. One is from Hong Kong, China, and the other from Paris, France. I was so impressed that those two young women would leave their homelands, friends and family, and travel so far to teach the gospel that I asked them for their testimonies. They are very bright, they speak the English language well, and they also write it well. I found that Sister Ho is the only member of her family to join the Church, and she did so against severe opposition from family and friends after seven months of study and prayer. The other is Sister Kopp whose parents are LDS and she has a strong testimony also.

I'm Sister Kopp. I'm twenty-one and I'm from Paris, France. I've been out on my mission a year. I was raised in the Church, but at the beginning, my parents were Catholic. They had just married and one day two persons knocked at their door. The missionaries introduced themselves, and when my parents saw they represented some religion, they weren't interested. However, because the fellows were Americans, they invited them into their apartment. They told the missionaries that they had to be to work in fifteen minutes. After a while one of the missionaries looked at his watch and said, "We've been here more than fifteen minutes. We'd better go and let you go to work." Both my parents were disappointed to have them leave so soon and asked them back. About two months later, my parents were baptized.

How grateful I am for having the wonderful opportunity to grow up in the Church. When I was young, I followed my parents and acted according to the testimony of my parents.

When I was about eleven years old, I was the only member of the Church of Jesus Christ in my school. These children did not have the same beliefs I did. They put a lot of pressure on me to do worldly things as they were doing, but at that time I could rely on my parents' testimony.

As I grew older, I knew that if I did not gain a testimony of my own, I would not have the strength necessary to live according to the gospel standards I'd been taught, for the pressure to break the commandments increased. I realized that everyone has to be converted to the truthfulness of the gospel, whether or not they have been born and raised in the Church, or they cannot withstand the temptations they will encounter to live in the world and yet not be of the world.

I decided to ask Heavenly Father if the Church was true so I would know for myself and not have to rely on my parents' testimony. I spent a great deal of time kneeling in prayer and studying the scriptures to find an answer and gain a testimony.

As I asked in prayer I heard something telling me that the commandments were true and to keep the commandments. I was rather confused because I didn't understand this answer so I prayed again and again and again; the voice kept telling me to "Keep the Commandments." Then, when I'd hear a talk about the Church or read the Book of Mormon, I'd get this great feeling that would flood over my entire being that told me it was true. It was like a great warm blanket that encircled me. I realized that no man could have written the Book of Mormon, no matter how brilliant. Each time I prayed, I heard the voice say the same thing. It took me a long time to understand that this was my answer, for I wasn't expecting this kind of answer. I thought Heavenly Father would tell me that the Church was true, but I came to understand that this feeling that flooded my heart of its divinity and the admonition to "Keep the Commandments" was my answer. Heavenly Father was telling me to keep the commandments because the commandments the Church teaches are true and good and would lead me to live righteously.

Since I realized that, my relationship with God is so much closer, and each time I read the scriptures or go to Church, I feel the Spirit of Heavenly Father testifying and confirming that His Church is true. This great feeling from the Holy Ghost strengthens my testimony. I know that this gospel is true. I would not have sacrificed so much to go on my mission if I did not know this for a surety.

I pondered a lot before accepting my mission call because to be a missionary isn't a responsibility to be taken lightly. It requires a great deal of sacrifice, such as: leaving my homeland and going to a strange country; being far away from my family; a lot of money; being far from friends; no TV; no dancing or dating; lost time at school because during a mission school stops; wearing dresses every day; walking and knocking on doors every day; forgetting myself—I could continue to make a long list of sacrifices.

But when I look at all the blessings I've gained through serving the Lord, I cannot count them. There are so many. They far outweigh the sacrifices that I have made! Among them are: sharing my testimony; love for others; knowledge of the scriptures; a better understanding of the role of Jesus Christ in my life; better understanding of the atonement; a closer relationship with God; learning to put my priorities in spiritual things rather than in temporal things.

I would like to end by saying that I know God and his son, Jesus Christ live and that they love us. They have prepared a wonderful plan that if followed, will bring us joy and happiness in this world and in the world to come!

I know that the Book of Mormon is the word of God and that Joseph Smith was a Prophet of God, and that our present prophet, Gordon B. Hinckley, is called by God to lead this Church and give us counsel. In the name of Jesus Christ, Amen.

Testimony of Sister Ho

My name is Sister Ho. I was born in Hong Kong, which is part of China now. My family are not members of the Church. My father doesn't even believe in a God or religion. We never talked about God or religion in our home.

I attended a Christian school from age six to eighteen, therefore, I learned a lot about the Bible. Since I was six, I have known that God loved me and all of the people in the world. I always knew that I could return to live with him one day, but the question was: what do I have to do to return to Him and what am I supposed to do to gain eternal life?

When I was thirteen, I started to go to a gospel study group with my friends at school. Actually, I loved discussions about the gospel, but I never attended any church seriously. I guess I didn't find any church that I enjoyed attending.

One day two men knocked at my door. They were LDS missionaries, and meeting them was a turning point in my life. I still remember that I met them during the summer when I was fifteen. They said they were members of The Church of Jesus Christ of Latter-day Saints. They asked me if I believed in God. I replied that I believed in God and in Jesus Christ. They also asked me many questions about my family, school, and friends. They seemed like very nice people. I talked with them for about thirty minutes at the door.

Three days later, two lady missionaries came by and shared the first discussion with me. They also gave me the Book of Mormon. I took this book to school and asked my friends and religion teacher if this book was true. They said it wasn't true, and they were totally opposed to me meeting the missionaries again. They said they were nice people but their beliefs were not true. I finally agreed with them so I decided to call the sisters and tell them that I didn't want to meet with them again. One of the sisters heard what I said on the phone but she didn't feel upset. She encouraged me and supported me until my heart was softened. I finally changed my mind about not letting them see me again, although it took about thirty minutes on the phone for her to convince me to let them come again.

Sister Ho and Sister Chow came to visit me the second time but they looked different than the first time. I guessed they were nervous since I originally called and told them not to visit me again. I could feel that Sister Ho really cared about me and never gave up on me. Most important, I loved her attitude so I listened to them. I had no doubt that they were nice people, but I still had the question in my mind if the LDS Church was true. When they invited me to be baptized, I couldn't accept until I knew that this strange gospel was true. *I decided to fast and pray and ask Heavenly Father if Joseph Smith was a prophet of God and if the Book of Mormon was true.* The missionaries kept asking me if I didn't feel the Church was true. I told them that I wasn't sure. For me, joining the Church was really serious. I wanted to make sure the Church was true so I would be dedicated with my whole heart. Otherwise, I wouldn't take this risk.

The sisters kept visiting me and inviting me to attend Church. I finally went to Church, and I'll never forget what happened that day. I attended a baptismal service. The missionaries sang, "I'll Find You, My Friend." When I heard this song, my tears started to flow and I couldn't control myself. My heart was totally touched by their singing. I kept thinking in my mind, "What's wrong with me?" Sister Ho could read my mind. She said, "Do you know what happened? You felt the spirit touching your heart." I didn't say anything but I have started recognizing the Spirit since that wonderful experience.

Because of this experience, I continued going to Church, but I began to feel such intense opposition from my parents and Christian friends at school that it was hard. My parents thought the Church was not a good church. They'd heard the Mormons used to have seven wives. Mother had heard many bad things from her friends. But in spite of that, Mother loved the missionaries, for she felt they had accepted a great challenge to leave home and come to a strange country to serve missions. She also thought it a good thing for them to learn another language, but she didn't want me to be one of them.

The point of view of my friends was different. They said the LDS Church was not a true church. They copied thousands of papers which talked about incorrect doctrines in the Mormon Church, and gave them to me, and they wouldn't meet with the missionaries to have their questions and challenges answered. All the material they gave me was written from the point of view of other Christian churches and they were totally against the LDS Church.

I told myself that I needed to make the decision by myself and not let others influence me. Sister Ho and Sister Kinnard continued to visit me for four months. (Sister Kinnard was from Colorado.) I loved them a lot. They were transferred and two new missionaries came. They were Sister Yue from Hong Kong and Sister Zardus from Wyoming. They invited me to have the discussions again although I'd had six discussions with the other missionaries.

During those discussions, they challenged me to be baptized. They said they'd fast and pray for me. I decided to fast and pray and ask God seriously. I knelt down in a quiet room where I wouldn't be disturbed and prayed to God with all my heart. I fasted that day with a purpose. I desired a testimony. I asked God if the Church of Jesus Christ was true, and such a Spirit of truth and light filled my heart that I knew without a doubt that it was true. I no longer had any doubts in my mind and I was willing to accept it with all my heart!

A few days later, I asked my father if I could be baptized. He asked me if I was serious. I told him I was, so he told me to ask my mom.

I was pretty nervous about asking my mother, but I prayed and asked God to strengthen me. She asked me the same question my father had asked. "Are you serious?" I replied "Yes! I want to join the Church. I know it is true!"

She said that I had to be sure I was making the right decision. I replied with a clear mind, "I am sure this is a right choice."

Finally, I was baptized on the 28th of March 1993. I was so happy to be baptized into the true Church. I had been investigating it for seven months. My family came to my baptism. All the missionaries had become good friends with them.

I know the Church is true, and that Jesus is the Christ and he heads this great Church. I know without a doubt that the Book of Mormon is true, and that Joseph Smith was a prophet of God as President Gordon B. Hinckley is today.

Now I am a missionary serving in the Utah Provo mission. I love sharing this wonderful gospel plan of salvation with others. I bear this testimony humbly in the name of Jesus Christ, Amen.

We All May Have Personal Revelation

There comes a time in each life when you have to confront your own beliefs and gain your own testimony, regardless of whether or not you've been raised in the Church. That time came to me as a young person because I was confused by having a wonderful father who was a non-Mormon and a loving mother who was a staunch Mormon. I didn't know what to believe so I decided I had to know for myself.

I gained a testimony by following the admonition of Moroni in Moroni 10:4-5 of the Book of Mormon, and I believe that anyone who sincerely wants to know the truth of this work can gain a testimony the same way.

I was baptized a member of the LDS Church when I was eight years old in a baptismal font in the basement of the tabernacle in Vernal, Utah. The tabernacle has now been made into a beautiful temple. I can still remember how chilly the water was and how rough the cement floor was on my bare feet. I realize now that they had no way to heat the water and probably brought warm water in, which soon cooled off, so no wonder it was chilly. I can still remember how determined I was to do nothing wrong from that time since my sins had been washed clean. Soon, I had forgotten my resolve and was quarreling with my sister. I remember thinking sadly that all was lost. As a child, I didn't realize the power of the atonement and repentance. How grateful I am to Jesus Christ that He atoned for our sins, or we would all be lost.

Mother was a stalwart Mormon; Dad was a non-Mormon, although a wonderful father and an important and well-thought-of leader in the community. He supported Mother in her Church work in every way, always attending Church whenever we children were in a program. He also contributed to the purchase of the Church organ, gave other donations, and stood up staunchly for Mormons and the Church whenever it was attacked as it often was in Colorado where he owned a ranch and ran sheep. According to my brother, Roy, a man was making fun of the Mormons one day and Dad said, "Warren, you don't know what you're talking about. When Mormons live their religion there aren't better people on earth. I should know, I've lived among them for forty years. He also would say fondly of Mother, "Mormons can't be very bad; Mother's a Mormon." It was still confusing to me, as a child, to have a mother whose whole life was the Church and her family, and a father who evidently didn't believe in the Church enough to join it. I was the baby of the family and my father's pet so I adored him and thought him perfect!

The daughter of a family who lived near us was my best friend, and they were stalwart Mormons. I often heard the children say that they were a "Forever Family." This made me feel like an orphan, for I knew we weren't.

Mother always took us to Church and as I grew older, I graduated from Seminary. Later I attended BYU where I met my wonderful husband, Fred Washburn. Even though we were married in the Logan Temple, occasionally a nagging doubt would creep into my mind. Was the LDS Church really true? If so, why hadn't my father joined? *Finally, I decided to take the advice in Moroni 10:4-5, where he tells us how we may receive a testimony. "And when ye shall receive these things, I would exhort you that ye would ask God, the Eternal Father, in the name of Christ if these things are not true; and if ye shall ask with a sincere heart, with real intent, having faith in Christ, he will manifest the truth of it unto you by the power of the Holy Ghost."*

I studied the Book of Mormon and prayed sincerely to know whether or not it was true. Nothing happened immediately, but one day I awoke to the realization that I really knew the Book of Mormon was true. *I didn't hear any voice or have any great manifestation, only a sure knowledge that it was true. I knew it as well as I knew my own name. It was a revelation to me to know without any doubt that this wonderful book was true, and that the Holy Ghost had revealed this to me! All doubt had fled!*

I realized that if I knew the Book of Mormon was true, I knew that Joseph Smith was a prophet, for he'd brought it forth. Since it testified of Christ, I knew He lived and was the Son of God. I also knew that this Church was true and it was His Church, and that we are led by a prophet today.

Since that time, I've believed that anyone who sincerely wants to know of the truthfulness of this work can follow Moroni's admonition and they will know. I am not a special person, but I had a sincere desire to know if this Church was true.

My father had always been immersed in business and extremely busy and didn't seem to be interested in studying the gospel. Although it was the great desire of Mother's heart that he join the Church, she didn't nag him or try to force him to join.

Sometimes God has to humble us to get our attention, be it through illness, losing one's life savings or other means. My father became seriously ill and so had time to contemplate the meaning of life and of eternity. He also took time to read and study the gospel. One day a good friend, Judge Charles Carter, came to him and asked him if he wanted Alice, our mother, and his family in the next world. He said "By all means. That is the great desire of my heart." "Then you'd better join the Church and be sealed together as a family," the Judge said. "You were only joined 'until death do you part.'" Daddy soon joined the Church, much to our great joy. He said later that he wished with all his heart that he'd joined the Church and become active in his younger years. I realize now that he could have gained a testimony many years before if he'd only taken the time to study the gospel. Nothing is gained without effort and a sincere desire.

I've always felt that it was a great loss to him and to his family as well as to the Church that he'd not accepted the gospel before, for he was a leader in whatever endeavor he undertook. This really bothered me that he'd not accepted the Church when he was well enough to be active. He died at age sixty-seven.

Years after my father's death, I was in a fast and testimony meeting when a sweet older lady in our ward, Sister Sarah Martinsen, stood to bear her testimony. This is what she said:

In the late fall of 1931, my husband, George H. Martinsen, was working at Elk Springs, Colorado at a sheep-shearing corral for Pitchford and Jensen.

The scaffold George had to use was not nailed properly. George was standing near the top when it gave way. He struck his knee on a piece of post, breaking his hip and causing him other injuries. He was brought home and put in a cast by Doctors Christy and Frankee. It was during the depression and he had been so glad to get employment, but due to the fall, it had only lasted a few days. Pitchford and Jensen carried no insurance. They came to our home and gave us a few dollars and that was all the compensation we received.

George was bedfast for four months, and we had seven children, some in school and two small children at home. I had the full load of nursing him and caring for the family. Winter was approaching and our food was running out. Things looked desperate in spite of the help we'd received earlier from the Church.

One Saturday afternoon, I sat by the window mending, fighting back the tears and praying silently and fervently to the Lord for some way to get food and fuel. I couldn't let George or the children know how utterly desperate our circumstances were. Suddenly a pickup truck stopped in front of the house and a man and his son came staggering up the walk under the weight of a tremendous load of a quarter of beef. They made several trips bringing a sack of flour, potatoes, and everything we needed, including coal for our stove.

The man was Clarence Showalter and his son, Don.

"I heard that George had been hurt, and I thought you probably could use a little help," he said. "If you or the children need anything else, go to Ashton's store and tell them I sent you."

I thanked him with all my heart, for I knew without a shadow of a doubt that the Lord had heard my prayers and sent kind Mr. Showalter and his son to help us in our time of need.

If ever there was a direct answer to prayer it was that day. Oh, how we enjoyed the wonderful beef roasts and stews I made with that delicious beef. Mrs. Showalter even sent milk, cream, and eggs to us. We lived like kings for the rest of the winter with that help until George got on his feet again.

I'd always heard how generous Mr. Showalter was, although I'd never known him well. God uses good people all over the world to answer prayers, and he surely used him to answer my prayers.

I had always known that my parents were extremely kind and hospitable. Dad's parents were southern and he had their example of southern hospitality to follow. No one ever came to our home around mealtime without being asked to dinner. My good-natured mother never complained for she was a marvelous cook and always had good food ready.

I was happy to hear this testimony that confirmed the fact that Father loved his fellow men and had charity in his heart, and had gone quietly about helping those in need.

I'd never heard before that Dad had helped the Martinsens, but I knew that he'd financed a business for two brothers—Bill Newton who was blind and his brother, Ike, who was a cripple. Bill had learned to make saddles while in the School for the Blind, so Dad set him and Ike up in a saddle-making and leather goods shop. They later branched out into making cinches and sent saddles and cinches all over the world. Eventually they became very prosperous. He also set up another man in a shoe repair shop which thrived and made him and his family a good living.

There was a bachelor, Henry Kurtz, running one of our ranches. Whenever he came into town, he knew he was welcome to come to our place, take a hot bath, have a good bed and enjoy Mother's delicious cooking. My parents treated him just like one of the family. Father got him on his feet financially, and later sold the ranch to him.

Father considered himself to be a hard-headed business man. In reality, he was very soft-hearted. He had one "Achilles heel." He simply couldn't pass up a hitch-hiker. The problem was that he saw many hitch-hikers on his numerous trips to Colorado to oversee his herds of sheep. Not only did he give the hitch-hiker a ride, but when he found him to be broke, he'd bring him home, feed him and give him a bed. "These people are good people who are just down on their luck," he'd say sheepishly to Mother to justify his generosity. Or he might say, "It was raining and I couldn't leave this poor person out in the rain."

I remember he once brought home a man and his wife, Slim and Alta, fed them and gave them a bed. Alta worked for Mother and he took Slim out to the sheep camp. They were with us for years and worshiped the ground Dad walked on. Some of those he befriended weren't so honest, or grateful, but Dad kept on helping them regardless. There is a scripture in Mosiah 2:17: "When ye are the service of your fellow men, ye are only in the service of your God." Perhaps God will forgive him for not being active in the Church and remember his deeds of kindly service, as we hope He will forgive us all for our shortcomings.

Whenever I think of my father, I think of the poem, *Abou Ben Adhem*.

> The angel appeared to Abou and Ben asked,
> "What writest thou?" The Vision raised its head.
> "The names of those who love the Lord."
> "And is mine one?" said Abou. "Nay, not so,"
> Replied the Angel. Abou spoke more low,
> But cheerily still and said, "I pray thee then,
> Write me as one who loves his fellow men."
> The angel wrote and vanished. The next night
> It came again with a great awakening light,
> And showed the names whom Love of God had blessed,
> And lo! Ben Adhem's name led all the rest!

Notes

Notes

Notes

Notes

Notes

0 26575 06782 8